Welcome to FLORIDA *(WTF)*

OUR JOURNEY TO PARADISE

GREG WINKLER

AND

VIKKI WINKLER

NEWMAN SPRINGS PUBLISHING
320 Broad Street
Red Bank, NJ 07701

First originally published by Newman Springs Publishing 2019

ISBN 978-1-64096-875-2 (Paperback)
ISBN 978-1-64096-876-9 (Digital)

Printed in the United States of America

(To the tune of *The Beverly Hillbillies'* theme song "The Ballad of Jed Clampett" by Paul Henning.)

> The Kinfolk said Greg move away from here,
> They said Flor-i-da is the place you ought-a be
> So we sold our house—and packed the SUV.
> Swimming pools, endless summer
> No more Wisconsin—not really a bummer

CONTENTS

AUTHOR'S THOUGHTS

Life is a journey filled with many different roads to travel and choices to be made. Each road leading to a different destination exposing us to different outcomes. We often share these experiences with others who may be on the same path for the time being. As we meet and intertwine with different people along the way; some enhance our experiences while others may put roadblocks in our path. Some of these people stay connected throughout our life while some are only there to help in a time of need.

The stories you will read about in WTF may seem familiar to you because a parent, a grandparent, a friend, or a colleague may have made a similar journey. You, the reader, may already be in Florida, or in another state because of a similar situation and reflect on the path you or your loved ones choose.

It is important to remember that things that seemed tragic at the time, like Vikki's first ant-bite, become humorous stories as time passes. As Vikki and I continued to refine our tale, our adventure, we would hear similar stories from the people we met at work or at the Tiki bars along the way. There is often a connection formed when you share similar experiences and those moments encouraged us to keep plugging along with the manuscript.

The other important thing we hope you take away from this tale of our adventure is that you realize and discover what "your beach is." Verbalize it, plan for it, and do it! We did not make this decision because the grass was greener (well technically it is because we are in the tropics now), we made the decision because it was where we wanted to be. Decisions like this can be difficult, there are always friends and family that may be left behind. While moving from loved ones is tough, with technology today we are only a facetime away, and we offer a pretty nice getaway spot for them to come visit.

Enjoy the read, laugh with us, feel our pain, and share with your friends. When you are finished you will realize what people really mean when they say, "Welcome to Florida". WTF!

1

The Dream

It is common for people, no matter where they live, to envision traveling and even relocating to a place of their dreams. Pillow talks with your significant other of just packing up all your belongings and setting off on a new adventure are dreams many couples share. Many will plan a vacation to their dream destination, totally enjoy themselves, and even look around the area at housing or possible jobs. Then the holiday ends, and they fall back into the life that is comfortable to them. The weather gets bad, the situation starts to get stagnant, and those talks start up again, sometimes even taking on a more serious tone. These talks almost, if not always, fall into the dream category, and then one day you look at your partner, you're seventy, and you wonder why you never took the plunge. What held you back from just taking that chance? How could your life have been different? For many, you will never know. For those that followed that dream, we may never hear from them again.

In our case, my wife, Vikki, and I, our dream spot was Florida. That state that puts "Endless Summer" on their license plate was always the destination of those pillow talks. The beach was still calling out to us. We both had traveled to Florida as young kids on many family vacations. We remembered the free orange juice stands at the side of the road, the e-ticket rides at Disney, and collecting seashells on the seashore. Our honeymoon, not by coincidence, was in West Palm Beach, Florida, and we beach hopped every day.

As our family grew from two to six, we would plan a vacation every four years with our four boys (I am a teacher, it took us four years to save up enough for those vacations—sorry, boys). The vacations we took every four years, you guessed it, were to Florida. We experienced Disney, Universal Studios, and the beaches of St. Petersburg and Clearwater. On one of those vacations, we rented a six-bedroom house for a week near Orlando, with its own screened-in lanai and pool.

"Best vacay spot ever!" the boys exclaimed. We saw all the beautiful things that Florida wanted us to see.

As we entrenched ourselves into our Wisconsin community, while battling the brutal six sometimes eight or ten months of winter, we would continue to have those dream talks of uprooting and moving to Florida. As each of our boys graduated high school, moved on to graduate college, and took real jobs, those dream talks started to feel more realistic. When our youngest was in his final year of college, our decision made. It happened! OMG!

The combination of three brutal winters in a row, the educational climate in the state of Wisconsin, a job prospect, and an early retirement option pushed our plan into hyperdrive. I applied for a teaching license in Florida and started looking for possible employment. How hard could it be to find a job in Florida? The Northern work ethic is a definite draw. Employers in the South love hiring Yankees because of that work ethic. I realized that didn't apply to teaching because it was difficult securing a position when there is over a 1,200-mile gap between your living quarters and the job. Many school districts in Florida have been "burned" by hiring teachers from out of state. Many teaching applicants are excited and accept a teaching position and then get cold-feet and never show up or even call to decline the new job. These experiences make it more difficult on those of us that are serious.

When we started to tell a few friends that we were looking to make *the* move, none of them took us seriously. Like most people, they thought we were verbalizing a dream. Overall, we kept our job search pretty quiet. When the goal finally became a reality, it was a massive shock to everyone we knew. People often talk about living somewhere else, heading to a beach, and changing their life. Few follow through. A plan like that was scary yet exciting at the same time.

After obtaining my Florida teaching certificate, a process in itself, we sat down and plotted out our plan to "Escape from Wisconsin." We set our goals, researched the area of the state we would like to live in, and started to search internet sites for jobs.

Job?! Why would I need a job? Although I was able to retire from teaching in Wisconsin with thirty years in the retirement system, I was still only fifty-four years old. Insurance is not in most retirement packages, plus the fact we wanted to maintain a particular lifestyle required that at least one of us obtained full-time employment. As teaching and coaching were still a passion of mine, I did not want to do it on the frozen ground anymore, and the reality of spending two-thirds of the year indoors. Wisconsin weather is unkind, and very, very cruel.

The winter before our escape from Wisconsin, the weather was ferocious. We had three weeks where the high temperature did not get above zero. We were out of school for three days in a row with a wind chill of -50 degrees. If you have never experienced that cold, it is hard to fathom. Just going outside for any length of time can kill you. Vehicles do not start, school buses do not run, and the streets are quiet since no one ventures out in those extreme temperatures. Vikki and I binge-watched *Breaking Bad* and decided we needed to *get out*!

Looking for a new job in a different state is not an easy task. I was beginning to think my age was a deterrent as I pursued a teaching position. I am an energetic and successful physical education teacher and coach. However, my white hair, or possum blond as my barber once said, made me look older than I behaved. To go along with the fact that many employers question the seriousness of your inquiry when you live 1,200 miles away.

While it is true that Florida has a massive teacher shortage, many of those positions are at poor-functioning schools and with certifications that I did not possess. I looked for physical education positions, not realizing that the physical education requirement for students in Florida happens to be a joke. The high school physical education requirement is *one* semester of physical education and *one* semester of health. So they created a course called HOPE, Health Opportunities and Physical Education. A school was not required to provide any other opportunities for PE except for that class. Students who do not want to take PE in high school can take the course online in the summer after their eighth-grade year and never have to step foot in a gym their entire high school career. Seriously, do you believe the stuff thirteen-year-old students record in an online class? These unmotivated students are asked to monitor and record steps on a pedometer as part of the online hope class. Once again, would you believe everything a young teenager tells you? WTF! Welcome to Florida.

At the time of our move, the climate in Wisconsin toward public education was changing, and not for the better. Our governor was ripping apart the excellent educational system Wisconsin was known for. Florida's scholarly reputation was weak as well, but that didn't matter to us; the location was the draw! When I began looking for teaching positions in Florida, the state ranked forty-fourth out of fifty for median salary. Wisconsin was ranked seventeenth, and that median salary was ten thousand dollars per year higher than at the Sunshine State. When I asked my new athletic director why the teaching and coaching pay was so low, he pointed to clear blue sky and spread his arms out—the weather! Of course! Thanks, seriously sunshine is lovely, but it doesn't pay the bills. WTF!

2

The Offer

Before our move to Florida, the boys' soccer season had already begun in Wisconsin, and I was excited about working with my new team. I did all the things I usually do when trying to put a team together, but I also had the Florida job pursuit on my mind. When I finished the opening practice of this new season, I discovered I had a voice mail on my phone. It was from the athletic director at a high school in Lakeland, Florida. He had called about the girls' soccer coaching position at their school. I also asked about teaching opportunities; he advised me to check their website and see what was there. He knew they had jobs in English and special education. I told him my certification was in physical education and I was not an English teacher.

"No worries," he said. They did not have any physical education jobs, but then he said, "You can take a test in any subject and teach in Florida." WTF?

At the time of this writing, Wisconsin required you to student teach in a subject before you could become certified in it. I say "at the time" because the educational system in Wisconsin was changing so rapidly people will not recognize it in a few years. Wisconsin had one of the best educational systems in the country. However, the current political movement made drastic changes; many of the standards put in place to help foster excellence are no longer required.

As I pursued a physical education position in Florida, I learned districts saved the high school PE jobs for football coaches. At this particular high school, my first stop in paradise, there were four teachers on the PE staff. The head football coach, the football offensive coordinator, the football defensive coordinator, and a female who was the girls' volleyball coach. A school of 2,500 students had only four physical education teachers, 75 percent of the staff being football coaches. Good ole boy network existed elsewhere, who knew?

When I later applied for a job in a Southwestern Florida county, I was informed by one assistant principal that the county had nine elementary schools and three physical education teachers. Each teacher covered three schools, and the county was looking to add a teacher at each elementary school. The administration knew how valuable it was to have an actual physical education teacher on site, but that did not matter, it always comes down to funding. The governor cut the state education budget that spring, and those positions never materialized.

I then applied to several high schools advertising for soccer coaches, but those schools did not have any teaching positions available either. A few of those schools asked me to take a test so I could teach history, special education, or English. All I would have to do was pass a test. Then I could teach a subject that I didn't have any experience instructing? That's a big WTF! And that, believe it or not, is how we made it to Florida.

The high school in Lakeland needed a head girls' soccer coach, I was a pretty good candidate, and the need was immediate. The school asked if I could teach a special education English class, a position that would require me to take two tests, one in special education and one in English. There was a cost to each test, and after some consideration, I made a decision. There was extensive preparation needed for the test, and I would have to decline.

I called the athletic director back on Tuesday, the day after he initially contacted me. I told him I didn't think we could make this opportunity work. As much as Vikki and I wanted to get to Florida, there didn't seem to be enough time. My fall soccer season had already started, and the first day for teachers in the Wisconsin school district was approaching fast. The Florida athletic director was persistent. He informed me that his high school was going to be adding two reading positions. I was qualified to teach that subject and asked if I was interested in teaching intensive reading.

Seriously? Florida has a class called intensive reading for high school students? Remember, I was coming from the Midwest, our educational system was excellent, I knew how to read books, and we were taught how to read before we entered kindergarten. I had never heard of intensive reading. What would that class look like, and what would teaching it require? I learned that students in Florida had to take a reading test and in order to graduate from high school they needed to achieve a preset score. Those that did not pass would be required to take an intensive reading course until they passed.

When I pressed my future new athletic director about this class, he told me in all honesty he had no idea either, he came to Florida from Minnesota. He did tell me all I needed was a Florida teaching license, which I had. I would need to take some classes throughout the school year to earn my reading endorsement to continue teaching the class. I would be able to take the graduate-level classes through the district at no charge. However, the burning question continued to be: "What is intensive reading?"

My new athletic director told me he would do some more checking on the position and provide me with more details. I'm not sure he extensively checked the syllabus because he told me the course was done entirely on the computer and I would be in a computer lab. I would teach six classes and monitor them on a web-based reading program. That sounded outstanding to me; we would get to Florida! I would coach girls' soccer and during the day monitor students in a computer lab. That seemed like it was too good to be true. Sign me up!

To me this sounded like a glorified babysitting position, a position often reserved for football coaches. I felt pretty unique; they were offering a job like that to me—a soccer coach. I was beginning to feel really special. This is where WTF started to materialize.

Welcome to Florida!

The next step was a Skype interview with the principal and the athletic director. Four days later, on a Friday morning, my soccer practice was at 9:00 a.m., and my interview was at the same time. I would do the interview, have my assistant start practice, quick change, and sprint out of my house to get to practice on time. I put on a shirt, tie, and sports coat with my shorts on. I was worried they would have me stand up and expose my lack of pants—ooh, the silly things that worry us. The interview became delayed about thirty-five minutes, and finally they called. The pace is a little slower the farther south you travel. That should have been an early warning indicator, but as they say, hindsight is 20/20. Welcome to Florida!

Four minutes later it was over. I took off the suit top, changed, and went to practice. When practice ended at noon, I had a call from the athletic director. The interview hurdle accomplished, the next step was to convince the teacher in charge of the reading department to hire a coach with no experience teaching English, but I did have twenty-four years of experience as a physical education teacher. I also sailed over that hurdle. Bring on the fingerprinting and drug test. I was almost there!

The principal called the following Monday, just one week after my initial contact and asked when I could get down to Florida. It was August 18. The Florida school year started that day, and Vikki and I had to figure out our timetable? They needed a teacher as soon as possible, and I was in Wisconsin with a house to sell, a home to pack, a soccer season I just started, and my school year, up North, about to begin…when did they need me? How much time did I have? Vikki and I thought, *Are we crazy? What is going on?* Little did we know what was in store for us. WTF!

3

What's Happening?

Our friend's mother was interested in our home. She came over on August 18, looked over the house, sat down, and we listened to her offer. The price was agreed upon, and the sale would be complete without a listing and without a realtor. The next morning we contacted a title company and started the paperwork right away. The house was *sold*!

Vikki and I now had a closing date of September 12. In less than a month, we needed to have the entire contents our house and garage packed, all our belongings—where! The job I was offered and accepted was mine once I passed my fingerprint screening and drug test. I was prepared to go to our local police department and take care of this requirement when the principal from my new school called and asked how soon I could get to Lakeland Florida. It was my understanding they would have a substitute in my "computer lab" until I could get there. The plan was for me to arrive in the middle of September, which allowed us to close on the house. It would also allow us some time to pack and find an apartment.

When the principal said I needed to get down there sooner, I started to panic. There was no way we could move things along any faster. He then explained that my background checks and finger-printing had to be completed in Lakeland, at the district offices. I did not have to stay yet, I just had to do the tests. Then I could go back to Wisconsin and finish settling things there. So I discreetly scheduled another trip to Florida on Labor Day weekend, a flight in on Monday, testing on Tuesday, and a quick flight out on Tuesday night. This trip I did solo. Vikki stayed home and continued to pack while I went to finalize this new position.

It's odd to me that we don't have some national database of fingerprints that schools, police departments, youth sports organizations, etc., can tap into and do background checks. Having to take a flight across the country to physically take a fingerprint test seems pretty archaic in this day and age. With the technology available to us today, it was an expense I certainly did not need to incur.

There are a couple of options when flying to Lakeland, or Central Florida. Orlando and Tampa being the two most prominent airports. Whenever we fly, we attempt to book direct flights. If you're flying to Florida and you don't get direct, it's usually "Welcome to Atlanta" or "Hotlanta," as we like to refer to it. You want to avoid Atlanta whenever possible. We fly with Southwest for the majority of our flights, Atlanta being a hub, as well as a hub for many other airlines. This makes Atlanta the busiest airport in the United States. If there is a storm anywhere in the country and you are connecting in Atlanta, there is a good chance your flights will be affected. On this trip, I was able to book my flight through Southwest, direct to Orlando.

There are some things you need to know when flying to Orlando: (1) it is *always* busy and (2) the plane is *always* full! Orlando is the land of Mickey Mouse! Families are always vacationing to Disney. Therefore, your plane will be loaded with families going on vacation!

Vikki and I often fly with Southwest. We utilize their "no change fees," and their policy of no baggage fees have us sold. Whenever we go back to visit Wisconsin, we take an extra suitcase so we can bring back fifty pounds worth of great Wisconsin cheese, New Glarus beer, and sausage. Thank you, Southwest, for the eventual blockage of my arteries!

With Southwest, they have zone seating; you do not pick your seats. That means the day before a flight, twenty-four hours from the departure time, one needs to log onto the website. The closer you click the button to the actual time of your departure, the better zone number you get. So Vikki and I drop everything we are doing to push that button. Zone A is almost impossible to get unless you pay extra money, so when we get a low B zone, we are excited. If we get Zone C, we are bummed for the next twenty-four hours.

The first time I flew Southwest to Florida, I was so happy to get B24. I was in the second loading group and certainly guaranteed an excellent seat selection. It was time to board. They called business select—what is that? There is no first class! Then they called for anyone with special boarding requirements—what is that? Then I saw a long line of blue poles!

The wheelchairs in Milwaukee have a blue pole on them, I never really noticed the wheelchairs on my other travels. There are always a few on every flight, but you don't really notice them because there are not that many. On most flights to Florida, the blue poles will be noticeable. My father-in-law always said he did not want to live in Florida because it is "heaven's waiting room." The number of elderly people that live and travel there is usually higher than most other states in the country. Often, the elderly need some assistance, therefore the incredible numbers of blue poles!

Well, now the blue poles are on, so I am ready to line up for my B group, but wait! The next announcement asks for any families traveling with small children. Remember, I am flying to the home of Mickey and Minnie Mouse, the flight is full of young, excited children. My B selection finds me in the back next to the bathroom, in the middle seat! WTF!

When I'm traveling alone, it really doesn't matter where my boarding number falls. There are always middle seats available close to the front of the plane. Then there is "the Southwest switch" that takes place with couples and the zone seating process. One partner will sit by the window, and the other partner takes the aisle, leaving the middle seat open. As a solo flyer, I scan to see which of these open middle seats have two people that appear to be the same age and friendly with each other. When I pick one and start to move into the aisle, it is amazing how quickly one of the people will move, opening up the window or the aisle. I foiled their plan; they had hoped to get a row to themselves. I am happy, I am up front and not in the middle.

I made my Labor Day weekend trip to Lakeland, paid $50 for my drug test and another $38 for the fingerprinting, and flew back that night. Then it was just a waiting game for the results to come back so the school district could offer me a contract and I could officially put in my two-week notice. It's funny how a person who doesn't do drugs and has never committed a criminal act can still be worried about a little background check. We again didn't tell anyone we were leaving because anything could happen with test results 1,200 miles away.

A little note on fingerprinting and drug testing, Florida does not have access to a national database. They don't even utilize a statewide database to track those that are tested. After my year in Lakeland, I was hired by Florida SouthWestern State College, their main campus located in Lee County. I was drug tested in Lee County for the college, with the college absorbing that fee. My teaching assignment was at their collegiate high school in Charlotte County. Charlotte County required another $50 drug test and $38 fingerprinting fee. I was offered a coaching position in Lee County and had to get fingerprinted once again for another $38 for the Lee County School District. After inquiring, I found out that none of those fees go to the perspective school districts. Background checks are a state mandate, and those fees go to the state coffers. Why develop a central bank to monitor those employees that are fingerprinted when you can profit every time someone gets a new job? In two years I was drug tested twice and fingerprinted four times. WTF! Vikki also had to endure three rounds of drug tests and fingerprinting for a substitute teaching position in several counties, just another "tax" for the state with no income tax.

Prior to finishing up *WTF,* I took on a new coaching position in the same county I currently teach. Before officially offering me with a coaching contract I had to make one more trip to the district office for another drug test, forty dollars more to the state coffers. I think it is awesome that the state wants to make sure there are not drug addicts and criminals working with their children, but you really can't come up with a statewide database?

The process of selling our house went so quickly and painlessly for us that I was able to enlighten you about flying to Florida. You also have been provided information on the background check process should you ever find yourself in a similar situation. We were able to sell our house without the expertise of a realtor, saving us a few more dollars before our departure. The closing date came, the keys changed hands, and we were out! My last day as a resident of Wisconsin, September 13, 2014.

4

Getting Out of Wisconsin

Honey, I got a job! Let's go to Florida! Oh wait…we have a house to sell, we have to leave our jobs, we have to pack up a lifetime, and we have three weeks to do this? WTF!

As I mentioned earlier, during this interview process, the school year in Florida had already started. Florida starts school the first week of August, and Wisconsin doesn't begin until after Labor Day. Before I could officially be offered the position, I was required to fly to Florida for a drug test and fingerprinting; that process needed to be in person. There was also the challenge of finding somewhere to live without knowing anything about the community we were moving to. Suddenly our dream was becoming a reality, and we started to feel overwhelmed with the task before us.

We told our immediate neighbors about our desire to escape Wisconsin; while they were reluctant to see us leave, they said their mom might be interested in our house, as mentioned previously. Their mom was in the process of selling her own home. She had already put an offer in on a different property. She had to move and soon! As soon as I learned about a job offer, we told our friends about selling our house, and their mom somehow canceled her offer on the other property. Just like that, we had a deal! All the pieces were falling into place. It genuinely seemed to us that this new adventure was meant to be. Things were beginning to get real. The stress that comes with significant life-changing events had just skyrocketed.

Moving is never fun or easy, but it is even more difficult when you have been married for three decades and raised four young men. The accumulation of stuff is unbelievable! This move would be our fourteenth move in thirty-two years of marriage. We recently celebrated our thirty-sixth anniversary and hopefully there aren't any more moves on the horizon. We had fifteen days to clean, declutter, and store our life. We had a rummage sale, and Vikki utilized some buy-and-sell sites on Facebook to get rid of even more. We were moving from a fourteen-hundred-square-foot home with a basement (a.k.a. lower level underground), with six-hundred more square feet of living space and a two-and-a-half car garage to an eleven-hundred-square-foot apartment with an outside (3v3) closet for storage and no basement! We had not even seen the apartment yet, so we had no idea what to take or what to leave behind.

We rented a storage garage in Wisconsin. It was 10 × 20 with a very high ceiling, and we packed it to the rafters. It cost us sixty-five dollars a month. We held on to that place for a year and a half until we finally settled into our new home. We donated gobs of stuff to St. Vincent De Paul's and threw a ton of belongings away. We tried to even pawn it off on our boys! Moving is a great way to purge! We probably would have gotten rid of a lot more, but we were very pressed for time, and if we were not sure, we packed it up for another time. Little did we know storage in Florida is an entirely different experience. When we relocated from Lakeland to Punta Gorda, we rented a furnished house for six months while we built. That meant all our current possessions would need to be stored for that period. We were able to pack quite a bit in the garage at the rental as long as we could navigate a tight path to the back door, but everything else had to be placed in a storage unit. Rental space in Florida was double what we paid in Wisconsin for one-third of the space. We still had the rental in Wisconsin, plus two small units in Florida. We were paying over three hundred dollars a month in storage fees to store "stuff." WTF!

Side note, if you plan on moving to another state, sell everything and buy new stuff when you get there!

We packed up our house, we packed up our U-Haul, and we were ready to hit the road. The process of obtaining the job, selling the house, and the quickness of it all certainly made it seem like we were on the right path. Everything was falling into place nicely, like this was our plan all along. We were excited, scared, and apprehensive all at the same time.

We were ready! The U-Haul was packed to the brim with a trailer attached carrying our SUV, which was also totally packed and ready to go. We even had some potted plants in the driver's seat. We planned on leaving early on a Friday morning. As we checked everything over on Thursday evening, we noticed a tire on the U-Haul trailer was flat. That minor setback was a foreshadowing of a more significant problem down the road, but how were we to know?

We called the hotline, and the U-Haul fix it crew would be out to remedy it Friday morning. Waiting for service only delayed our departure time by three hours. Not a big deal, right? And that was the beginning of our U-Haul adventure.

Note to self, there are other options. No more U-Haul rentals for us!

The tire changed, we said our goodbyes, again! Our journey to paradise was about to begin. I turned the key in the ignition, and nothing happened! There was no spark. I tried turning the key again, and still nothing happened. Let's do this! One more time…bingo! It fired right up. Here we go! Was there a reason for the truck not starting? I questioned this in my head for a moment, but we were already behind. "Let's go, honey. Florida, here we come!"

We were finally on our way, but we had to stop occasionally. I'm lying. We had to stop almost every two hours. Vikki needed to pee—a lot! (She's better now.) We left Wisconsin and made it around Chicago without any major delays—that was shocking— and we crossed into Indiana. We finally had to fill up, so we pulled into a huge Love's Truck Stop. Filled up, grabbed a snack, and went out to continue our journey. As I turned the key, nothing happened. Oh no! What was wrong? I continued to try, nothing. I googled it, tried again—nothing. Vikki went to the trucker entrance and asked a driver. He gave us a recommendation, nothing. Time to call the U-Haul hotline, again!

U-Haul would send an on-call mechanic that would arrive in forty-five minutes. Two hours later he showed up, with a child in his truck, a small child. He looked around the ignition and then entirely dismantled the steering column and finally determined it was the ignition switch. He did not have a replacement with him, so he merely took out the entire ignition and cleaned it up! Another two hours later, the truck started, and we were good to go. He said it should get us to Florida, try not to turn it off and on too much. "Ahh, okay," we answered, with confused looks on our faces. Finally, after four hours in a Love's gas station bay, we were back on the road. Our next stop was to be a hotel near Nashville for the night. At this rate, we would get there at 1:00 a.m. We called to tell them we may be late—we never made it.

It was nearing 11:00 p.m. We needed gas, again. U-Hauls suck the money out of you. We had a gift card for a BP gas station. It was dark, and we were about two hours from Nashville when we pulled off the highway because we saw a BP sign. It was a little blip of a place on the map, somewhere in Hicktown, Indiana. The BP was closed, but the pumps were operational. A quick fill-up, and we could get back on the road. I made a mistake. We are always told to shut off the vehicle while pumping gas. Well, I should have left the truck running. After filling up, the truck failed to start.

In this little Hicktown location, the BP was a meeting spot for every postteen high school student with a pickup truck or a motorcycle. As I was attempting to contact the U-Haul hotline, once again, the BP lot was beginning to fill up. There were a bunch of interesting-looking characters smoking cigarettes and drinking out of paper bags starting to assemble at our closed-for-the-evening BP. They were keeping a pretty good eye on us as they kept squealing in and out of the parking lot. Their trucks would fly down the road, burn a quick doughnut, then speed back to the lot. It was quite unsettling and a bit intimidating to be sitting in the pump bay with your entire life in a truck and hauling our car on an attached trailer.

The people on the U-Haul hotline were being very difficult. They advised that someone was on the way, but it would take at least two hours. They asked us if there was a hotel close. They could put us up in a hotel if it was a Best Western, a Holiday Inn Express, or a Hawthorne. There was nothing in the immediate area. I frantically tried to continue starting the truck as we waited. The stares from our gathering were becoming more and more uncomfortable. It was like watching a flock of turkey buzzards circling fresh roadkill and waiting for it to expire. We were that roadkill.

I kept trying to turn the key, hoping our truck would jump to life. And then I heard the engine beginning to purr. We were almost in disbelief, but it was true. The vehicle was running! I put the beast in gear, and we hit the road.

We had to cancel our original hotel reservation because we weren't going to make it to that destination. We called the U-Haul hotline, again. I was able to get the same person who I'd been dealing with after our initial breakdown. They were not happy that we left the increasingly dangerous location of Hicktown. I advised the agent that we were going to try and find a place on the south side of Nashville, off the highway, where they could send a mechanic in the morning. Originally the agent had told us our rescue mechanic would be coming from Nashville, so I thought I was doing a good thing. For some unknown reason, our agent was not happy that we bolted.

The hotline agent calmed down and confirmed that U-Haul would put us up at a Holiday Inn Express if we could find a room. A few hours later we found one, pulled into the lot, left the truck running, and went in to check availability. It was 2:00 a.m.

Our U-Haul contact asked that the Holiday Inn Express send them a fee sheet. They would take care of the room, and we could sleep until our truck was fixed in the morning. What a relief! We parked the U-Haul out of the way, turned it off, and went back to get the key to our room. In the meantime, our U-Haul agent was replaced by someone else at the call center, and now our room was denied. We spent the next four hours in the lobby of the Holiday Inn Express arguing with the new U-Haul agent. We were not sleeping and not in a room! Fortunately for the U-Haul agent, Vikki was feeling sick and developing laryngitis. I could read her body language, and with a voice added to those gestures, it would have been ugly!

At 6:00 a.m., they agreed to the room charge. We slept and woke up at 8:00 am. The truck was fixed by 9:00 a.m., and we were on our way to Florida. We had two hours of sleep and needed to get to Lakeland that same day as I was supposed to start my new assignment the next day. We were exhausted!

After the U-Haul incident was finally over, we disputed the $2,000 truck rental. A representative called and negotiated it down to $500, an amount we considered reasonable for our trouble and inconvenience. Unfortunately, six months later, they reneged on the agreement, and the additional $1,500 showed up on our credit statement. As I referenced earlier, we will not be using that company ever again. We have used Penske numerous times since, and they have been outstanding!

It was a long drive from Nashville to Lakeland, I believe we arrived at the city limits around 1:00 a.m. I had been in touch with my new principal during our ordeal, and my start date was delayed by a day. That was a blessing. We still had to unpack enough of the truck to be able to sleep that evening. I think we collapsed around 4:00 a.m., with a lot of unpacking ahead of us the next day. Our first night, we grabbed our pillows, a few blankets, and slept on the hard floor of our new Florida apartment.

We had booked Vikki on a flight back to Wisconsin that evening. Vikki was still working in Wisconsin for the next two months. The school district I dedicated my life to did not accept my retirement and instead changed it to a resignation. That minor play in semantics took away all of our health insurance benefit, so Vikki had to work a bit longer until our new benefits kicked in. We kept a vehicle there for her. She bunked with my parents and was still sick and miserable, not because of her living arrangements but because we were 1,200 miles apart and our climates registered a significant sixty degree difference. It wasn't paradise if we weren't together.

At least one of us was in Florida! Vikki finally decided to say "screw it, I'm moving to paradise too!" We purchased catastrophic insurance for one month and wrapped ourselves in bubble wrap until my new policy kicked in. It was a long month for both of us waiting for Vikki to drive back down so we could start this new chapter of our life together. She had a friend ride with her when she finally made her escape from Wisconsin. They got lost a few times and experienced a few adventures of their own along the way. When she finally arrived in Lakeland, she had no idea where to go. She had only been there once, and it was late at night so already dark. She was not used to some of the multilane intersections and drove the wrong way on a one-way street. It was the eight-lane intersection of 570 and 37. That was a precarious situation. She was stressed, tired, and freaked out. There was a "blue light" on the traffic signal. She was sure she was getting a ticket in the mail. (She didn't.)

The two of them quickly pulled over, found a sushi place, had some sake, and allowed their nerves to settle; it wouldn't be long before I came and rescued them. I had been across the state in Miami. I had met my oldest son at the Packer game. I was not at the apartment to greet them. Several phone calls and a few sakes later, I found her. She was here, we were back together, and she was exhausted. I was turning a Florida reddish brown, and she was ghostly Wisconsin white—that would change!

5

Driving in Florida

Living in Wisconsin, when the geese started to fly south, we knew that winter weather was on the way. Here in Florida, we're not concerned too much about winter because as the license plates say, we have "The Sunshine State" and "Endless Summer." We do know when winter is on the way not because the geese show up but because the snowbirds start to arrive. To be politically correct, this group of people should be called "winter travelers." No one said I had to be politically correct, so *snowbirds* it is!

Snowbirds are people that migrate from the brutality of winter, people from the East Coast, the Midwest, and any other cold and gloomy state in the US and Canada. Snowbirds flock to Florida for the warmth, the umbrella drinks, the beaches, and the golfing that sunny tropical Florida has to offer. A standard joke in the pistol-shaped state says, "You know it's fall in Florida when the license plates start to change color." Vikki and I didn't technically fall under the snowbird category for very long because we moved here. We did, however, contribute to the changing of the season at first.

The latest statistics show that the Sunshine State has over a thousand people moving here on a daily basis. Where are all these people living? Add to that the large numbers of snowbirds, approximately one million people per season that flock to Florida. With those numbers you can start to imagine the traffic congestion that peaks from Thanksgiving to Easter. This brings me to another WTF experience—poor drivers and auto insurance.

Of course, one of the first things we did after settling in was to call our insurance agent and change our car insurance. A simple and easy task, we thought. Maybe there was a possibility that our rate would be a little lower. We felt because we no longer had to worry about deer running into our car or the icy roads of winter, a cheaper rate would be waiting for us. We did not realize that driver's education was a "suggestion" for teenagers and not a requirement. The rural teens have grown up driving ATVs and swamp buggies, but the kids that live in town do not get that kind of practice. When we received our first Florida car insurance bill, our jaws dropped to the floor.

Our insurance premium more than doubled from our previous payment. How in the world could that be? For one, Wisconsin requires higher driver education requirements for teenage drivers. The other primary reason for higher rates in Florida brings us to be the number of drivers on the far end of the age spectrum. There are many silver foxes driving vehicles. On some of my first cruises down Tamiami Trail, I saw what looked like driverless cars. Then I looked over into the car I was passing and saw a tuft of white hair just above the driver's window.

Florida has an aging population, as I am starting to experience that process. There are many new surprises ahead for us, one of those being the compacting of the spinal cord, which leads to a lower number on the height chart when we visit the doctor. Some of our population now has trouble seeing over the steering wheel. Often when traffic is slow, it could very well be due to the compressed spined drivers cannot see the speed limit signs.

Like my wife when she drove down the wrong way on Hwy 37 in Lakeland, many of the snowbirds, newly relocated, and vacationers are unfamiliar with the roads. This leads to sudden stopping and unsafe lane changes. Couple those people with young, driver education–less teens and this creates a recipe for vehicular disaster. Thank you, Geico, for making me pay for this!

Traversing the Tamiami Trail, Hwy 41, will teach you a lesson in patience. At one time, this was the only way to go from Tampa Bay to Miami, a four-lane, often six-lane highway that takes you through all the Gulf side towns: Venice, Sarasota, Port Charlotte, Fort Myers, Cape Coral, Naples, and Punta Gorda, to name a few. Tamiami Trail is lined with businesses, many car lots, malls, bars, and restaurants. Did I fail to mention the *traffic lights*! (We used to call them stop-and-go lights). If you had an unlimited amount of time, you could follow Hwy 41 from Florida all the way back to Wisconsin—I don't think that's happening!

The traffic lights are equipped with extremely long timers! You certainly need to have an island "no worry" attitude when you're driving in the Sunshine State. At one intersection, my wife painted her nails, on both hands before the light changed and we moved on. There are many accidents at these intersections. I think it is because the drivers fall asleep waiting for the light to change! They startle awake and rear-end the person in front of them. Drivers also step on the gas to get through the yellow lights because they know if they don't make it, they are sitting long enough to worry about shaving again. And can someone please tell me why drivers slow down for green lights? When food is dropped on the floor someone always yells "five-second rule" and you are free to still eat it. At the traffic signals when someone yells "five-second rule" it means you are waiting at least that long until the car in front of you moves after the light turns green.

There are many theme parks and attractions available in Florida. If you are looking for adventure, this state will not disappoint you. Unfortunately, driving anywhere will be one of those adventures. Before my long career as an educator, I was a city police officer in Wisconsin. I am thankful every day for all the defensive driver training they put me through. It certainly comes in handy.

As you drive around, you may also start to wonder if car manufacturers include turn signals in the vehicles they send to Florida. Drivers change lanes here like they're the only ones on the road. There is seldom a signal for a lane change or turning for that matter. Many of the roads have two and three lanes each direction. Vehicles fly down the roads, weaving in and out of the traffic lanes like they are participants in a NASCAR race. When I asked one of my police officer friends about people here using turn signals. "Welcome to Florida" was his response.

If you genuinely want to experience driving at its finest, then I-75, the I-95, or even worse, I-4 is the place to be. I-4 is listed as the worst highway to drive on, records the most accidents, and it is located by a popular tourist destination. You guessed it—Disney! It will amaze you how traffic can be flowing along at 80 mph and suddenly come to a standstill. You crawl along for fifteen minutes and then back to 80 mph. No accident, no police stop, no dead alligator in the road, just a phantom *stop* and *crawl*. It is very perplexing.

In the glossary, you may have looked at the term *gawker*. Most of us know what a gawker is, but in Florida, on the highway, it can be disastrous. The reason for many of the sudden stops along the major roads will almost always be due to gawker traffic. There can be a small fender bender on the opposite side of the highway, and traffic will come to a standstill on both sides of the road. People can slow down to look at a dead alligator carcass, and it will tie up traffic for miles. It is such a weird and annoying phenomenon, and very frustrating.

As I was reviewing this chapter, Vikki and I had taken a day trip to Matlacha (pronounced Mat-la-shay), a unique little artsy community on the way to Pine Island. When I asked Vikki if she wanted to visit, she thought I was introducing her to some new friend. We walked around, visited some shops, and bought some local art. We decided to drive around Pine Island and see if there was anything else to see. Pine Island is a Marine community, no beaches but abundant opportunities if you're a fisherman or a boater. We are neither, so we went to the end of St. James City, turned around, and headed for home. As we drove on the two-lane road, traveling at the posted speed of 55 mph, we came to one of those phantom stops. This time someone up ahead was making a left turn and waiting for a break in traffic.

We slowed, then stopped. I looked in my rearview mirror, and that is when I saw it. A vehicle was still flying down the road, bearing down on my rear at 55 miles per hour! There was no time. It happened so quickly, and I was waiting for the impact. The seventeen-year old driver slammed on the brakes and managed to point her car toward the shoulder. I felt a slight nudge on my rear bumper and watched a car fly by me on the shoulder. Vikki has a vivid picture in her mind of the teenager's face as she whizzed by our car. The image of the girl's ghostly white face and deer-in-the-headlight look, of course holding her phone as if she had been texting, is slowly fading. We were lucky, a little paint off the car, no injuries, and a lesson learned for the driver.

As we were checking out the car and exchanging our info, this young lady said she worked at a car wash and would take us there. She could get us a free car wash and buff out any scratches for us. We followed her to this popular destination on Pine Island road and received a free wash and wax, and the young lady buffed out the scratches. What a strange day. What could have been a significant disaster ended with a free car wash! WTF!

Inattentive driving is the primary cause of accidents in Florida and probably everywhere. Whether texting, talking on the phone, or just daydreaming, the traffic stops so suddenly here that as a driver, you always have to be aware. The sheer number of people in the state and the number of vehicles provide traffic nightmares for engineers. Teenagers do not have to go through extensive driver's education in Florida like they may be required to in many other states.

I wonder if Florida offered defensive driving classes? A class for turn signals and maybe a booster seat for people over eighty? Maybe we could get the insurance rates lowered? Yes, we do have year-round sunshine, but we also have higher insurance rates, and you take off a month of your life at every traffic signal. WTF.

Welcome to Florida!

6

Two Wheelin It

I'm an avid cyclist, not a biker. I prefer to use my quads for propulsion. Cyclists, I'm learning, are not well liked on the Florida roads. You wouldn't guess that if you're a visitor to the state. There are many "bike friendly" communities with miles and miles of bike paths and "Share the Road" signs everywhere.

Our first stop on the relocation to Florida was the booming metropolis of Lakeland. Lakeland is a growing city smack-dab in the middle of Orange Juice country. Polk County, which surrounds the thriving city, has corporate offices for Geico, Publix, Amazon, and many other growing businesses. It is a community with an identity problem. They think they are a metropolis, but in reality, Lakeland is a large rural town that has exploded in population. When we were starting to relocate there, I checked out the city's webpage. Lakeland was listed as one of the best cities in Florida for cyclists. I was excited!

Lakeland boasts many miles of bike paths, all wide, paved, and relatively safe. For the recreational cyclist, one could get a ride in with very little vehicular interference—that is, if you load up your bike and drive to a parking lot with the bike path access. There are also some nicely marked roadways and a nice bike lane that loops you around the downtown. Many small lakes provide homes for numerous swans and other fowl, so it is quite the scenic ride. I'm sure this is the reason they received the best bike community designation.

I utilized many of these paths during my year-long stay in the community. While riding on those pathways, I experienced a flat tire at least once a week. When I finally got tired of changing my flats, I took my bike to the local bike shop to see if I needed new tires. I found out that Polk County, like many counties, use ground-up tires to make their blacktop. The bands in the steel belted radials get ground up, which makes it impossible to remove all the little wires. The heat and wear on the bike paths push these tiny steel fibers up through the blacktop, and they almost *always* found my tires.

Most cities now have bike lanes between the vehicle lane and the shoulder. Many of the routes I pedaled on in Lakeland, had lanes that took me around the beautiful ponds. The bike lanes also contributed to many of my flat tires. There are a high number of traffic accidents in Florida, leaving broken glass and debris on the roads that are not always cleaned up. The daily summer and fall rains push the broken glass and debris down into the low spots of the roadway, which also happens to be where the bike lanes are, thus causing my magnetic tires to attack more sharp objects, like glass and pieces of the broken car, which gave me more opportunities to change my tires.

My rides tend to be longer than the fifteen-mile bike path could provide me, so I would often venture out onto the country roads. I managed to find some roads that didn't have a lot of traffic but always enough traffic to keep me on my toes. Did I mention that there are a lot of people living in and visiting Florida *all* the time? Every road I went down had my favorite sign, the one that featured a bicycle on it and the printed phrase: "Share the Road."

I quickly learned that pickup trucks were not my friend. A pickup truck on a Florida country road, in my opinion, often is driven by a camo-wearing Flo-grown man. Many times this said pickup had more than one occupant, empty beer cans in the bed, and a Rebel flag flying off the cab or a Rebel sticker on the rear bumper. My observations and road-riding experiences have led me to believe that when you buy a pickup truck, they make you sign a pledge, a promise that when you drive by a cyclist, you will get as close to the rider as humanly possible without touching them.

It could also be possible that the driver and his merrymen are intimidated by a white-haired man in his late fifties who still wears spandex. It could also be they are Florida Gator fans, and I often wear a Florida State University cycling jersey. Whatever the case, anytime a vehicle encroaches within my three-feet of roadway, there seems always to be that black-and-red Rebel flag waving somewhere on the truck. Not that there's anything wrong with that! (Seinfeld reference.) WTF!

After we left Lakeland and headed to the Gulf Coast, many of the same experiences I had in central Florida were evident by the coast as well. There are well-marked bike lanes on the main roads and some great bike paths in the cities and towns that pop up all along the coast. The growing population of Florida makes it a given that similar cycling problems are in every community. A cyclist will always have to watch out for the drivers who are well past their prime, sitting on their booster chairs, and still behind the wheel. There are still many rural pickup truck owners just waiting for the rider to leave the city limits and get out onto "their" country roadways.

On one occasion, on Hwy 17 heading east to Arcadia, while riding in a well-defined bike lane, I was pushed into the shoulder by a semi, who after buzzing me decided to drift over into the bike lane even further to let me know it wasn't an accident. As I was about to one-finger salute him, I saw the Rebel flag attached to the rear window of his cab. I resisted the urge to one-finger salute because Florida has a conceal and carry law, and I wasn't taking any chances.

WTF. Welcome to Florida!

One final cycling story for your reading enjoyment. I was using my bike to commute from our rental in Punta Gorda to my teaching assignment. It was three miles to my place of employment, and I could utilize sidewalks the entire commute. I always wear a helmet when I train, but when I commute, I tend to go slower, and my headgear is a baseball cap. It's a leisurely ride. I often ride with no hands and drink my morning cup of coffee as I pedal. On this particular day, as I was about to leave school, the familiar Florida weather pattern was about to dump copious amounts of rain upon us in a short amount of time. Some intimidating clouds were moving in, and some intense little storms were popping up. In Florida, when it rains, you're told you either wait five minutes or drive five miles and everything changes. I figured I could ride fast, get home, and avoid Mother Nature's daily fury. I was wrong!

I started to ride away from school on the sidewalk when the heavens opened up and the rain came down in buckets. There were also a few lightning bolts, so I put the hammer down and started pedaling as fast as I could. I lowered my head into and aerodynamic position and tried to get to a nearby CVS Pharmacy to wait the storm out. It would be over in four and a half minutes, right?

The path had a slight curve with a large bush hanging over the sidewalk. The roadway was quite close, and the traffic was spraying up more water, so I grazed the corner of the bush with my left shoulder at close to twenty-two miles per hour.

Boom! Bam! Smash! Crash! All those things happened.

I was on the ground, flat on my face, and my left shoulder was throbbing. I could barely breathe, and my right side was in excruciating pain. I felt like I was back playing high school football, and I got blindsided by a massive linebacker without wearing my pads. I had no idea what just happened. The rain was pouring down around me, and I had just done a face plant. As I lay there, not moving, I was doing a mental self-check. My head was okay; my right arm was extended and in severe pain. I moved my arm slowly, aware that collarbones are susceptible to breaking in bike crashes. The initial physical self-check of my condition was telling me nothing was broken and I could get up and move.

After continuing with my self-assessment, I got to my feet and then checked out the bush that I hit. It was not a bush! It was a cemented mailbox in disguise! The residents appear to be over-zealous landscape people. I'm assuming they did not want an ugly mailbox dotting their landscape, so they planted shrubbery around this cement bike killer. I limped to the corner CVS with broken ribs and some road rash. When I arrived at the CVS, I managed to get my phone out and call Vikki. After laughing nonstop for at least an hour, okay, maybe five minutes, she could not believe the bush I hit was a mailbox. She wanted to take me to the walk-in clinic, but I had experienced broken ribs before. There is nothing they can do for them. To make things more complicated, I wasn't familiar with our new insurance yet.

So we didn't go to the doctor, nor did we report the accident. Broken ribs have to heal on their own and on their own timeframe. I did try to contact the mailbox owner's by sending them numerous letters asking them to please trim their "mailbush-box." To this day they still have not responded. I should have called an ambulance. I point out the scene of this accident to all of our visitors when they come like it's a local landmark. Everytime I bike near that residence and see that *mailbush,* I have PTSD, and I secretly give them a one-finger salute as I pass.

Just another WTF moment in Florida to add to the list.

7

The DMV

Everyone has a story about their DMV, Department of Motor Vehicles. It's no different in the state of Florida. Only in this state it's referred to as *the tax collector*. As if the DMV wasn't scary enough, now you call them the tax collector? Even more intimidating!

So you move to a new state, and of course, you need to change your driver's license and vehicle plates. It's certainly not an easy task; the hours are 8:00 a.m. to 5:00 p.m., Monday through Friday, similar to a typical workday for most, which means I have to make plans to go there on my day off. The prudent thing to do is go online and see what type of documentation you need when you enter so they can process your needs quickly. Vikki and I did that, and we decided we would change our driver's license first. Actually you have to change your driver's license before you can change your plates. We heard awful, scary stories about registering our vehicles from others that came before us, so we grabbed our current driver's license, proof of residence (our electric bill), and of course our checkbook, and then it was off to the ominous *tax collector*.

We discovered when we arrived at the tax collector in Lakeland, that it was a ginormous building. We walked inside to a reception desk; we spied a large waiting room to the left and another of equal size to the right. Security guards and metal detectors greeted you first. The building was packed with a big screen above the reception desk with the number of the next customer. Adjacent to the waiting rooms were double doors leading into another room with over twenty little cubicles. Once your number was called, you were able to go to the cubicle assigned to your position in the waiting room.

After waiting for quite some time, we were excited when our number popped up on the screen. We went in to see the attendant and provided our materials. The clerk was pleasant, looked it over, and asked for another form of ID. We had given her our Wisconsin license, showed her credit cards, and family photos. She explained that Wisconsin was one of twenty states where the driver's license was not recognized in the state of Florida as a valid ID! What? Can you repeat that? We needed our social security card, birth certificate, or marriage certificate. WTF! Are you kidding me? Of course, I carry those around with me all the time! After waiting so long, at least an hour, and with our apartment over a half hour away, we were not going to make it back by five o'clock. Our trip to the tax collector would have to wait until the next time we had a day off.

A month later, we ventured out again to the ominus *tax collector*. Same process, had the correct paperwork, and a few hours' wait, new driver's licenses for each of us, a hundred dollars to the tax collector, and we were on our way. A much easier process the second time around! Next up would be our two vehicles. According to the law, you have ten days from the time you start a job, to change your vehicle registration. We had now been in Lakeland for six months and decided we better get the plates changed before we went to jail for the terrible crime of not registering our vehicle. Our vehicle was registered in Wisconsin and we had four more months before it expired, so technically our vehicle was registered, just not in the right state. The positive thing for us is that it was still snowbird season, so there were more out-of-state plates than Florida plates at this time. However, we are law-abiding citizens and thought we better take care of our responsibility.

We gathered up our required paperwork to make a trip back to the tax collector to register our first vehicle. Believe it or not, we experienced a problem—again. The vehicle we were registering was paid for without a lien. Proof of insurance and the title was supposed to be in the computer system. For some reason, we didn't have a paper copy of the title. The attendant searched for it online but couldn't find it. We couldn't proceed, so once again we left and waited for another day off to come back. During that time we called and made a trip to our bank and obtained the necessary paperwork. We then planned another excursion to the tax collector and finally changed the plates of one vehicle. Florida charges a tax per weight of the vehicle, a fee for a new plate, and then a standard $225 for an initial Welcome to Florida (WTF) fee. We left with our checkbook $350 lighter, and this was only for one car! We repeated the process the next month. Finally we were driving legally in paradise, or so we thought.

While relocating to Punta Gorda, I took a little trip to Englewood Beach, and I was stopped by an officer. I was unaware I was exceeding the posted speed limit. You cannot blame me, though; there were two exceptionally lovely-looking women biking in some rather skimpy bikinis. I digress. The officer issued a warning, I wasn't from around there, but the officer noticed my driver's license had a Lakeland address. He told me I had ten days to change the license or I would get fined. Even worse it could be jail time!

We had a dilemma; we were living in a rental while our home was being built. If we changed to our current address, the rental, we would have to change it again in six months. That was a little silly and redundant. The officer was friendly and advised that as long as we had a physical address of the build, we could use the address of our new home. When we took care of our new driver's licenses again, all that existed at our future address was a large slab of concrete.

It was time to visit the Charlotte County *tax collector*—again!

8

Promises, Promises

This is actually where the "WTF - Welcome to Florida" idea was born. My first teaching job in Florida, the promises, the misinformation, the perception, and the vision of paradise almost shattered. On the first day of my new job, at my new school, while teaching a totally new subject matter, I wondered if we made a mistake. I walked into a waiting classroom, found a teacher's desk, no computer, no grade book, no attendance lists, and absolutely no direction. When I went to the reading teacher down the hall, who was to become my mentor for intensive reading, I asked her about my lack of materials. The first response I heard out of her mouth was, "Welcome to Florida!" Every time I went to her with questions or for some clarification, she always had the same response: "Welcome to Florida."

As you may remember, I was sold on the teaching position because I was going to monitor a room full of students in a computer lab while they engaged in a web-based learning program. Walking into my classroom on that first day, I started to question my sanity and asked myself what I had gotten myself into? The first reality check hit when my computer lab—I mean, classroom—did not have *one* computer in it. There wasn't even one on the teacher desk. This was a shock, and questions started to flood into my head. Also missing was a class syllabus or instructions, not to mention my class lists or a schedule. I sent a message to my athletic director (this was his fault, of course) asking if it was possible to get a class list and a class schedule. You may be thinking to yourself, why did I contact the athletic director and not the school secretary?

To help you understand a little, I was officially hired after Labor Day. I didn't start until September 14 while the students in Florida start classes in early August. They had been taught/monitored by a variety of substitutes during the previous four weeks. Shortly before the end of my first period, on my second day of teaching, the class lists and a schedule were delivered to my room. I was promised a computer by the end of the day (it showed up three days later). To my dismay, the schools in Polk County followed a block schedule (one-hundred-minute classes). My former school had fifty-minute classes. I was now teaching a new curriculum, and my classes were way too long for the subject matter. Have you ever attempted to keep high school kids engaged in a class they hated for one hundred minutes? Well, let me be the first to tell you it's an almost impossible task. Add to the fact that I now had to actually try to teach the subject matter instead of just play on a computer. My ordinarily low stress level was starting to climb. What have we done?

This new school was large and designed like a college campus with seven different buildings, spreading out the faculty. Each of the buildings were connected with an awning to allow you to get from one to another without getting drenched if it would rain. The block scheduling didn't provide a lot of time to meet other teachers, and I felt like I was alone on an island. There didn't seem to be a lot of socialization within the staff, and it took some time to meet people and be included in their after-school get-togethers. The teacher assigned to help me was my immediate contact, and she fielded many questions from me the first few months. She became a friend and a valuable resource. Her initial responses to me were always the same—"Welcome to Florida!"

It didn't take long to figure out my class or the expectation they had for me as a new intensive reading teacher. However, I never did get that computer lab. At the start of the second semester, I received five computers in my classroom and had to figure out a system where my thirty students, each period, would have an opportunity to work on the same reading program. We had moved to Lakeland, Florida.

It was not paradise, and for the time being, we had to make the best of it. To make matters even worse, Vikki was still back in Wisconsin, and she had to work for another month before joining me.

Educational practices in Florida are much different than our experiences in the Midwest. A recent national ranking (Education Week 3/2018) had Wisconsin ranked thirteenth with a 78.8 score. Florida was ranked thirtieth with a score of 72.5. I was teaching students that failed to pass the state reading test as juniors and seniors. In Florida, students are required to pass the state reading test to receive their diploma. My class was, for some of these students, their last opportunity. If they didn't meet the required standard on that test, they left high school with a certificate of completion. WTF, I had never heard of such a thing.

Vikki decided to contribute to our finances by becoming a substitute teacher in Florida. In most Midwestern states, a four-year college degree (which she had) is required to become a substitute. If you want to substitute teach in Florida, you need thirty college credits to be employed. If a school considers you as a long-term substitute, you would only need an associate degree. Vikki was hired at the same high school I was at as a long-term substitute. She taught juniors and seniors in a reading course that had even lower-ability students than the ones I taught. Needless to say, not only are low-performing students not motivated, they become discipline problems as well. It was a rough six weeks for Vikki.

Vikki's biggest shock as a substitute was an experience in the classroom when she had students read a story about violence and shootings. A decade prior to our move we had an experience with our soccer team while we stayed overnight in a hotel in Milwaukee, Wisconsin. There was a shooting during the evening, two people died and two more were injured. Fortunately for us and our team, no one in our group was a victim of the crime. As Vikki was telling about her frightening experience, ten of her twenty students raised their hands. They began to show off their scars and tell stories of family members that were shot in their neighborhood. They enlightened Vikki about gang activity and drive by shootings in their environment. As I said, it was a rough six-weeks for Vikki.

To give you another example, one of my colleagues gave an assignment in English class. The students were to look at the alphabet and write one sentence that began with the letters of the alphabet starting with A and ending with Z. A student raised their hand and asked, "What? You mean we have to write thirty-five sentences?" WTF!

The coaching portion of my position was outstanding. It was a great team, exceptional young women, and the highlight of my days, but it wouldn't be enough to keep me there. I repeatedly asked my athletic director to help me find a physical education position in the area. I was passionate about coaching at the school, but without a teaching position, I would have to look elsewhere. The Gulf Coast was calling, and our job efforts would start to be focused there.

I left Polk County after one year for an opportunity that was a better fit for Vikki and me. On to our next Florida adventure!

9

I Get Paid What?

Coaching was my gateway into the state of Florida and the reason we were able to make a move at the time we did. After a three-decade career in Wisconsin, how much different could it be coaching high school soccer in Florida? It's the same game, the same age level, no problem, right? WTF!

School districts in Florida are huge. They are countywide school districts, unlike Wisconsin where every community is its own school district. My former teaching position was in a town with a population of forty-five thousand, had one high school, and was one school district. When we moved to Lakeland, Florida, the city had a population of one hundred thousand people located in Polk County. Polk County is one school district with thirty-six high schools. School funds have to be distributed equally between all those schools, including middle and elementary. The athletic budgets are bare bones, fund-raising, and tickets to contests are the primary sources of athletic income for underfunded athletic departments.

The first thing I asked my athletic director was how much money I had in my soccer budget. His response? "Whatever you want it to be!" What the—? My funds were unlimited as long as I raised the money. As I prepared for my upcoming season and my first parent meeting, I asked about the school's athletic code. I wanted to make sure the team was aware of the guidelines and rules. Most schools across the United States have separate athletic codes for athletes. Again his response was priceless. As he spit his morning chew into the trash, he said, "Athletic codes? We don't have any athletic codes. Are you kidding me? We wouldn't have football teams in Florida if we had athletic codes!"

Some of the cities are so large in Florida that students in those locations are assigned zones. Depending on the size of the community and number of high schools, eighth-grade students rank their choices for schools and then are placed after that school year. In Cape Coral, for example, there may be five high schools in one zone. At the end of eighth grade, you're told what school you will attend. You could live across the street from one high school and be placed at another. The crazy part for athletics is that you can request to switch schools, without moving, year after year. Families that have eighth graders in a club program together often seek a school collectively, so they keep a group of athletes together. I refer to this as high school free agency. WTF!

As I prepared my Lakeland team for our first home game, during that first girls' soccer season, I happened to be out of town for a conference on a Monday with the game that Tuesday. Our game and practice field doubled as the school's football stadium. The football yard lines were painted as they were still in season, but the soccer lines were nonexistent. I shot a text to my athletic director and inquired as to whether the field would be ready for the game the next day. His response, "Call me."

I called and was informed that measuring the field, placing the stakes, stringing the lines, and marking the field, were my responsibility! What? The school grounds crew didn't have enough time to prepare the football game field for soccer. The grounds crew took care of the football needs, but soccer was not their responsibility. My athletic director advised that if I didn't have time to do it, I could try and hire a parent to do it, again with no budget. That meant on the day of my first game, after school, I was out measuring, staking, and spray-painting my game field. Thankfully, I had some willing players to help. When referees arrived later that evening, they were a little concerned that I may have been under the influence; our field lines were quite wavy.

Travel was another issue. In the Polk County district where I coached, the team had to find their own way to our soccer contests. We seldom were able to secure a bus because the district utilizes the buses all day long. They used them for the high school, the elementary schools, and then the middle schools. Transportation wasn't available for athletics unless you were able to leave after 5:00 p.m., which very seldom worked for our team. The school rented a suburban from Enterprise for me on those days so I could maybe take six players. I gave the team and the parents the schedule and had to hope everyone would make it to the game. We were also not allowed to meet and have a caravan—Florida is a strange state. That law or practice continues to baffle me. I cannot drive more than six players, and they don't provide a bus, yet a seventeen-year-old student could potentially drive themselves to a game over sixty miles away. Of course, I was unaware that would be taking place. (Insert sarcasm.)

According to the director of the state coaches association, the retention rate for coaches over a four-year period is about 13 percent. Approximately a hundred thousand coaches enter the profession at some level each school year in Florida. After four years, only thirteen thousand of these men and women are still on the sidelines. I believe the main reason is a combination of the massive amount of responsibility placed on the coach, the lack of support, and indeed low pay.

Coaching is a supplement for a teacher. That means they get paid at the end of the season in one lump sum, and it's recorded as a bonus for tax purposes. So I can help you understand, as a soccer coach, I would start my season in mid-October and end sometime in late January. My coaching supplement was $2,000. My check, which arrived one month after the completion of my season, was $1,475.

Add to that the expectation that you have off-season conditioning before the season, again after the season is over, and also highly recommended throughout the summer. It's very hard for coaches to justify the time away from a spouse and a family when they are away that many hours with very little financial reward. It actually works out to less than $1.25 an hour. When I was twelve, I pulled weeds at a vegetable farm for $1.39 an hour. I sure have come a long way since 1972!

No worries, we are, after all, teachers first. Education across the country does not have the support it once had. Many, especially those that are retired or have no kids, question why so much of their tax dollars need to go toward education. It's an even bigger problem in Florida, where the average age in many coastal communities is over sixty-three. Elderly people on fixed incomes forget the value of education and the opportunities that schools provide for our youth. Some of that is why teaching salaries in the state of Florida continue to be near the bottom in the country.

According to recent US Labor Department statistics, the average teaching salary in the United States is $57,000. The highest state average in teacher pay would be the state of New York at $77,000. I left Wisconsin, ranked twenty-second in the country, with a state average of $54,535. The state average teaching salary in Florida, ranked forty-second in the United States, is a whopping $48,134. In Charlotte County, where I accepted a teaching position, they only recognized seven years of my thirty-plus years of teaching on their pay schedule, which put me at $42,000 per year. Add to that, my coaching salary of $2000, and I was going to make bank! ($44,000 per year). Health care for me was included, that's a good thing. Vikki had to be added to my health plan for an additional $600 per month, that turned out to be $7200 from my base pay. This book better sell because $36,800 before taxes will not be enough to stay in paradise!

It really makes no difference what state you live in. More and more demands are placed on teachers and coaches. An educated population is better for everyone, and as a country, we seem to have forgotten that. I have worked and continue to work with very dedicated individuals who could've been very successful in other fields but chose to be educators. As a parent or a grandparent, a little gratitude toward a teacher goes a long way.

10

The Season

My entire life has been dictated by seasons. When I was in high school, it was football season, wrestling season, track season, and then baseball season. As I started my career in education, that didn't change. In the fall I coached boys' soccer (the boys' season), in the winter as the assistant athletic director I covered basketball (basketball season), and then in the spring, I was coaching girls' soccer (girls' season). Vikki identified my coaching seasons as "soccer widow" season for her. We also had four seasons in Wisconsin: fall, winter, spring, and road construction—I mean summer. In reality, it starts getting cold in October, extremely cold and snowy December through February, then rainy/snowy cold until late April. Summer, at most, was three months, but generally we only had nice weather for two of the three months. Vikki was convinced we only had two seasons: winter and July! Vikki and I knew when we moved to Florida, our seasons would go away. It was the land of "Endless Summer," and we gladly embraced it!

Once we moved, we were confused when people would start talking about *the* season. We would go to a local restaurant, and if we agreed to meet friends at seven, we would get seated immediately at seven and enjoy a lovely evening. Our friends would say, "Just wait for *the* season." When visiting the beach, we would find a parking spot close to the sand and enjoy our time among small groups of people, and our friends would say, "Just wait for *the* season." A short drive across town to the mall commenting on how quickly it took and we heard it again, "Just wait for the Season." What are they talking about? What season?

We live in Punta Gorda, located on Charlotte Harbor. We have some great marinas and restaurants but not a real beach. Our closest beach is twenty-three miles away. When we visit the beach between April and early November, it will take about forty minutes. When Vikki and I are driving somewhere, our rule of thumb is, whatever the total mileage away—we double that for the trip time. The traffic lights are everywhere and impede our progress. When "the season" arrives, travel time can more than double. We were used to driving in Wisconsin, where a thirty-mile drive took thirty minutes.

Well, they certainly didn't mean hurricane season, although that is something we have to be aware of, as well. They were talking about snowbird season, and then it happens! Sometime around November, it begins. It takes longer to drive places, there's a long wait at our favorite restaurant, and the beaches are beyond crowded! The population swells and continues to grow until just after Easter and then returns to "normal" sometime in late April or early May.

Punta Gorda is a quaint little city with a registered population of around seventeen thousand people, that number triples during *the* season. Our closest major airport is Southwest Florida International in Fort Myers. Finding a direct flight in the off-season is often difficult. Southwest offers thirteen flights daily and very few of them direct. During the season, however, that offering shoots up to sixty-six per day, with many direct flights to destinations we like to visit. The economy is heavily stimulated during *the* season. There's live music all over town during happy hour, and the nightlife becomes more exciting and certainly more entertaining. However, you have to fight crowds everywhere and be patient when you go out to your favorite eateries or cruise around town.

Another unknown problem, until you experience it, during the season is a simple visit to the local post office. Punta Gorda has a fantastic little post office. I have never experienced friendlier postal employees than the staff in Punta Gorda. There is one postal employee that is so bubbly you have to double-check to see if you are really in a post office. She treats everyone with a smile and makes the wait in line seem shorter. Her personality is infectious, and it is transferred to the other postal counter employees.

The problem is that there is never a good time to visit the Post Office. Many of the residents have relocated from other states. They moved away from families and friends to live their lives in paradise. Then you add the multitude of snowbirds that visit, and all those people send packages home at an alarming rate. It's like Christmas season from November to May. There is *never* a good time to visit the window. It is just like waiting for the traffic signals; you need to be patient and go with the flow. If you are an impatient person, I strongly recommend you send your spouse or pay a local kid to run that errand for you.

You learn quickly, as a full-time resident, to make your doctor's appointments, oil changes, and bike repairs during the "winter months," which is actually summer. Recently, I made a new doctor appointment, and when I gave the secretary my address, the first question she asked was if I lived here permanently. From late May until early November, the local businesses get to take a sigh of relief and slow down a little. It's great to have so many visitors during *the* season, but it's also nice to have it quiet down for a bit.

11

Damn Yankees

When I told a friend of mine who was born and raised in this state that I was writing about the experiences on our journey to live in Florida, he was intrigued. Because he was born here and also raised as a rancher, he is a real Florida cracker. I told him I was writing a chapter called "Damn Yankees." He asked me if I knew the difference between a Yankee and a damn Yankee. I said I had no idea. His response? "The Damn Yankees—They stayed!"

This could be a sensitive chapter for some. Remember I was raised my entire life in the state of Wisconsin. Before my existence in this world, our country, the US, fought a civil war. That's correct, we fought against our brothers and sisters, and we fought against our fellow Americans. The war was primarily about slavery. Our president at the time, Abraham Lincoln, led this charge to abolish slavery. The divide in America during the 1860s was the North against the South.

The North, flying under the American flag, was in conflict with the South, flying under the Rebel flag. The North, which included Wisconsin, won this war. The Northern armies were known as Yankees, a title the Southerners continue to call people who come down from the North. Florida was one of the original seven states to secede from the Union after Lincoln was elected president. Therefore, Florida would be part of the Confederate or Rebel army.

In that period there were some Floridians that did not want to fight for the Rebels, and they fought for the Union. Despite the fact that the Civil War ended over 150 years ago, the Rebel flag still flies in many places across our country. Racism is still prevalent throughout the state of Florida, as it is in many others. This is especially true in the rural communities. The closer you look around the state, the more you begin to see a wide gap in the haves and have-nots in what many call paradise.

When you head to Orlando and visit Mickey, Universal Studios, or SeaWorld, the attractions and bright lights amaze you. If you're not visiting "the Happiest Place on Earth," you're probably on the Atlantic or Gulf Coast. The beaches are fantastic! The beach communities are beautiful and full of life. You may never venture West of I-95 or East of I-75, where the natives live. When and if you drive the backroads across the state, you'll start to see the extreme levels of poverty.

The Yankees, myself falling into that category, all moved to the coastlines where the sun and surf called us. You may see the Rebel flag on a touristy T-shirt in a local beach shop but you don't often see the pickup trucks with a huge Rebel flag flowing out of the back in these touristy areas. In my rural hometown, in Wisconsin, students were sent home from school if they wore the Rebel flag on a T-shirt, bandana, or belt buckle. Every morning, here in SouthWest Florida, one of my students is dropped off at the front door in a truck with the Rebel flag flying off the truck bed. When you start to spend more time in Florida, you find out how far apart we are in our beliefs as a country. You begin to see it within elementary schools located in the middle of disadvantaged neighborhoods. A hundred percent free lunch, and consequently extremely low test scores are prevalent. It's tough to excel in school when you're not sure where your next meal is coming from when you get home.

As I was driving to the Tampa International Airport one afternoon to pick Vikki up from one of her trips, I happened to listen to a talk show hosted by Drew Garabo, 102.5 The Bone. It was a very entertaining show. The topic of the day was the removal of a Confederate statue in front of the Tampa Bay City Hall. Drew entertained several callers. The majority of them were self-proclaimed rednecks. In my opinion, many of the callers were drunk when they called in, and it was three thirty in the afternoon!.

Most of the callers were not in the same opinion on the matter as Drew was, which made the show that much more entertaining. It was also pretty evident that a lot of what I heard about the Florida educational system was showing itself in this conversation. Remember, I was initially hired to teach a required class to graduate from high school called intensive reading. We did not have that as a class in Wisconsin because it wasn't needed.

One argument against moving the statue—to be more precise, they were not destroying the monument, they were relocating it— was to eliminate a Martin Luther King statue for every Confederate one taken down. So in essence it was turning into an us-against-them argument. If you really think about it, where have you ever witnessed a war that the side being defeated was still able to fly their flag? I'm pretty sure there are no longer any swastika flags flying in Germany, yet we allow the Rebel flag, a symbol of racism, to fly in the South. WTF!

12

Everything Is Trying to Kill Us

I was excited to begin teaching as I arrived for my first day as a physical education and health teacher at Florida SouthWestern Collegiate High School. My new principal gave me a tour of the facility and showed me my gymnasium. Well, there wasn't a gymnasium at the school. My gym consisted of an enormous outdoor green space. There were outdoor tennis courts, sand volleyball courts, a few handball courts, an outdoor basketball court, and of course my green space. Next to the basketball court is a walking path, which is located next to a wooded area. There are two signs off the trail, "Beware of Gators" and "Beware of Venomous Snakes." WTF!

Are you serious? My outdoor classroom, where the basketball court is, happens to be within five feet of a sign that warns me about things that will kill me? Where am I?

When I questioned the principal about the reality of a gator or a snake arriving at my class, he advised me that there is an occasional panther in the area as well! And quite possibly a bear! Was he serious? I called Vikki later that day, "Honey? Did we move to paradise or a jungle?"

We've realized that everything in Florida is trying to kill us. When I was coaching at George Jenkins, I went to do an inventory of my soccer equipment. The girls' soccer program had an excellent locker room away from the school with a coach's office and storage room. The location was behind the stadium and quite impressive.

I went there before the season started to inventory my equipment. As I moved the equipment bags, there was a slithering snake nestled between the soccer bags. WTF! It was multicolored, and I flipped out! I had never seen a snake with all those colors. I grabbed a corner flag post (actually just a pole with a stake in the bottom and a flag) and started beating it like hell! I felt like a real man! I had killed my first snake in Florida. My first thought was, *Can I get this mounted?* I took a picture and sent it to a science teacher back in Wisconsin to see if he could tell what dangerous species I had battled and conquered.

To my disappointment, it was a common rat snake. A friendly fellow I should've let live to help keep other vermin away from my supplies. I have seen numerous snakes since, near my house, out on my bike rides, and around the school. As far as I know, they're the harmless ones, and it's live and let live now. A little rhyme to help remember which snakes are safe: "Red against yellow can kill a fellow, Red touching black: Safe for Jack."

So how do you feel about gators? As a youngster visiting Florida with my parents, we would stop at the roadside stands that advertised baby gators and free orange juice. They were the cute little gators you could observe in glass fish tanks, gator claws to purchase, gator claw back scratchers, and gator heads to take home and put in your bedroom. The roadside stops advertised their gators like the prehistoric reptiles are harmless, contained, and mesmerizing! When you spend any amount of time in Florida, you realize these scary-looking creatures are everywhere! WTF!

If there's a freshwater pond, there's a gator. The large freshrives rivers that spill into the Gulf or the Atlantic are full of these long-nosed beasts. We have a neighborhood gator that lives in our pond. Gators do not like people; they'll avoid you unless they're defending their young ones. You should certainly not let your little dogs run free around a pond because they make a sweet midday snack for the gator. Do NOT attempt to feed the gators. When people feed them, they will return to the spot where they were fed for more food. If someone feeds them for a while, they come closer and closer to land. As they become comfortable, they will venture further into the yard where there has been a food supply. Recently a child was attacked and killed at a Disney resort because a gator, after being fed for a period of time, got comfortable and thought the young child was food. They're not friendly creatures, so it is wise to respect them. It's also advisable, if you have a pool, to check it in the morning before jumping in; I told you, if there's freshwater, you will probably find a gator.

We had some visitors fly in late one evening. After we picked them up, we pulled into our development, and our neighborhood gator was crossing the road! What a sight for our friends from the north. He was trying to get from one pond to the other. He just froze in our headlights, and we had to wait for him to decide whether to continue his journey or come and say hi. We often see him on the banks of the pond catching some afternoon rays. One afternoon we saw our neighborhood gator attack a large water turtle. The turtle was in the gators jaws and we observed the "death roll" as he killed his prey. Fortunately, when our gator is sunning itself on the bank, when a person heads in his direction, he quickly dives into the water and lurks just below the surface. Gators really do not like humans.

Frogs or, as my New York neighbor pronounces them, fraaags, are also entirely different from what we're accustomed. There are a variety of frogs that show up often on the lanai screen, in the house, on the house, and in every other nook and cranny. Most of the frogs and toads are quite harmless, but they leave their waste tracks on the outside of the house. When we get an abundance of rain, the number of these little fellows seem to increase. We are often surprised when entering our garage code on the outdoor keypad, by one of these frogs looking for shelter. The frogs show up on our car door handles and often under the wiper blades. Scraping frogs off the house becomes a seasonal task. There are some larger frogs and Cane toads that are dangerous and poisonous to pets. We try to keep an eye out for those nasty creatures.

The Gecko is another little creature that likes to roam around and say hi. We love these little guys as long as they stay out of the house. We call them geckos; real Floridians call them lizards. I like gecko better. They're fun to watch as they scurry about and climb on our lanai screen. We try to catch them and put them back outside, but their tails break off, and they get away. No worries, though, they grow back! A student of mine would catch them, and he had a way of making them open their mouth. He then had them bite his ear, and walked around with live Gecko earrings—WTF!

Florida is full of strange-looking creatures. We have crazy pre-historic-looking birds, bald eagles, armadillos, water turtles, and tortoises in addition to our gators and snakes, and that doesn't include the dangerous creatures in the ocean. Whether it's the wildlife or the insects, we're visitors to this tropical state, and there are many creatures that don't like sharing this sponge with us. And don't ever forget, we invaded their habitat, and they are all trying to *kill* us!

13

Ants and Bugs

Let me start by telling you that Vikki hates bugs! In Wisconsin, she would freak out about the little centipedes and the tiny insects that would roll into a ball and scuttle around in the dark, damp basements. The saving grace in Wisconsin was that our bitter cold winters would send most of the irritating insects to their demise. That is not the case in the tropical, sunny, and humid weather of Florida. Our move brought different bug experiences to our lives.

Probably the most disgusting bug in the world is the cockroach. Black, offensive, and revolting creatures that scurry in the dark and feast on garbage. Cockroaches were not little creatures we often saw up north. They usually existed in the garbage and dirty places, not places we often found ourselves—that is until we moved into our new apartment in Lakeland, Florida.

Lakeland is a large city, a hundred thousand plus people during the off-season, as I mentioned earlier. When the snowbirds invade, the population swells even higher. When we found out about my new job, I asked around about nice areas to look for a temporary residence, an apartment complex preferably. My new principal in Lakeland recommended a place within two miles of the school; he said it was very nice and he and his wife had rented there when they first moved to the area (a decade prior). We liked the proximity to the high school, and it was located in one of the more beautiful suburban sectors of the community.

The place looked nice online, the rent was a little higher than we had hoped, but with that cost, we assumed the clientele would be young professionals or people in similar situations to ourselves. There is always apprehension when you buy or rent something "sight unseen", you have to trust the information you receive is current. We were amazed to see some of the junk that started to pile up around many of the residents' patios—oops, I mean lanais. We were also concerned about the frequency that the unit above us and to the side of us kept changing occupants. We did have to sign a year lease, yet during that time, we had three different groups of people renting in the upstairs apartment.

One of the tenants above us had a smoking obsession. We kept hearing strange noises from the new second floor tenants. After an exhausting investigation, we finally figured out where this disturbance was coming from. It was the middle of June, and the air-conditioning was on. The outside units were right out our bedroom window; we thought *that* was our problem; it was not. Our upstairs smoking renters needed to take constant smoke breaks. Since lighting up in the apartment was against the rules, they would go out on their balcony to satisfy their need. The sliding patio doors were causing a sound that made you think a storm was coming and it sounded like thunder. It was annoying at two or three in the morning. As disturbing as the noise was, the disregard for our lanai below them was evident as their cigarette butts started to create quite a little trash pile.

While we kept our place in pristine condition, I'm not sure our neighbors were doing the same. If they did not care about what garbage they allowed to pile up outside, what did the inside of their apartment look like? The rental unit on the side of us produced a lot of noises, and we had no idea how many occupants were staying there. As we continued to clean and spray for ants, flies, and cockroaches, it never seemed like we were doing enough. In an apartment complex where cockroaches can breed, does it matter how clean your place is?

One night during the middle of the rainy season, Vikki got up to use the bathroom. It was probably two in the morning, and I had to get up at six to get ready for school. I heard a piercing scream, and my hyperventilating wife was beside herself in the bathroom. I groggily jumped out of bed and rushed to her aid. There it was—the biggest and ugliest brown bug I had ever seen! It was slipping and scurrying along the inside of the tub. I valiantly grabbed my shield, a sword, and a flip-flop to defeat the monster. I'm sure the crunch could be heard in the next county!

When Vikki told others of her horrible experience, they laughed and told her not to worry. It was only a palmetto bug. They were harmless and liked to be in dark, damp places. She calmed down a little until she googled what a palmetto bug really was: "Palmetto bug: Florida Woods Cockroach, grows up to 1.2–1.6 inches in length and can release a stench." This one had to be a freak of nature as it was, according to Vikki, at least three inches long. Well, that little definition put her over the top. The cleaning and application of bug spray just increased until we got ourselves out of there! After our unwelcome visitor, Vikki became obsessed with her search for unfriendly creatures. To this day she never goes barefoot; she is always wearing flip-flops.

Her next bug encounter was a smaller little beast but much more vicious. As we were heading out one evening, the car was parked near a grassy area, Vikki stepped on the grass wearing sandals and felt little stings on the heel of her foot. She did not see any creatures in the area and wasn't overly concerned about it. Later that evening, her heel started to itch, and little white blisters showed up. She popped them and started to scratch and scratch and scratch. The blister heads came back, and she scratched some more.

When she went to substitute teach the next day, the students were asking what was wrong with her foot. It was oozing yellow pus all over her sandal and the floor. These tremendous young minds told her they were bull ant bites, more commonly known as a fire ant. She had a bad allergic reaction to this creature's bite and still swells up immensely from them.

Once again she tried to identify where this mysterious bite had come from, and some locals explained that she had encountered her first fire ant. Living in the frozen tundra of Wisconsin, we had never been exposed to these tiny annoying and painful little creatures. I, of course, had avoided any contact and could not empathize with her ant ordeal—until I got a new job at Florida SouthWestern Collegiate high school in Charlotte County.

I was hired to be the HOPE teacher—that is, health opportunities and physical education. I was ecstatic to be back in PE! When I arrived on campus for the first time, I found out that they hadn't had a HOPE teacher for a few years. The prior grade took the course online. That meant that all the school's physical education supplies fit in one small storage bin. The grass area would become my gymnasium, and all my classes were outside year round. We have classes outside even when the heat index is over 105 degrees. In Wisconsin, we cancel youth sporting events when the heat index nears 100. I guess it's a matter of what you get acclimated too.

The first week, I decided we would play kickball games in that grassy area. I went to the maintenance department and borrowed their push mower so I could mow some lines in the extremely tall grass. They hadn't been mowing the area because no one was using it. Therefore my new gym had grass at least six inches tall. I started up that push mower and began making my lines. I had on my tennis shoes and some ankle socks. I started to feel sharp little stings all over my ankles. What was going on? I looked down at my feet, and they were covered in little tiny ants, and my feet were on fire! I started to do the ant dance and swat them off of me as quickly as I could.

It took a few hours before those tiny little stings started to itch and turn into small little pimple blisters. I scratched them raw, and the sores produced a yellow crusty puss. The itching and pain from those bites subsided about a week later, but the scars from my encounter remain with me today.

You would think I would have learned my lesson but a year later I was attacked again. This time I was coaching a soccer game at a high school in Fort Myers. We were playing a subpar team, and after going up 2–0, we found ourselves tied 2–2 at halftime. I met my team in the corner of the field at halftime. I was furious at my team! Well, not really furious, just extremely disappointed in our performance. A lesson needed to be learned. It was dark out, and the light was not real bright in the area where they sat. I proceeded to get their attention with my halftime motivational speech. That's when they struck again. Right in the middle of my rant, the ant dance took over again! The pain, the pus, the scratching, and the scars returned. Fire ants were all over my feet, ankles, and legs - I will certainly be paying for this. I have to do a better job of checking my surroundings! (Note: If you are attacked and bitten by fire ants, pour bleach on the bites, it will lessen the swelling. Yes, I learned this the hard way.)

Another annoyance Vikki and I are very familiar with is the mosquito. It is the state bird of Wisconsin after all! Okay, I lied, it's the American robin, but it should be the mosquito! Anyway, mosquitoes are annoying and prevalent when it is wet or the humidity rises. Often, though, you can hear them, and they are big enough that you see and swat them as well.

As we were moving into our apartment in Lakeland, after our horrendous U-Haul experience and on the road for fourteen hours, we learned of a new bothersome insect—the no-see-um! The no-see-um is a very small sand fly that inflicts the same amount of pain as the mosquito. The difference is that you never see them, hence their name. The bites are just as itchy, and often you are covered in them before you realize it.

As we were unloading our truck at 1:00 am that day, we were attacked by these creatures. This experience motivated us to pay an extra $1,200 to upgrade our lanai screen when we built our house. When we visit our neighbors and spend the evening socializing in their lanais, we will come home covered in no-see-um bites. It is always too late; we never see them. We prefer to have the neighbors over to our lanai after the sun goes down. At the very least we should remember to bring our insect repellant!

Vikki always has the worst bug experiences. One day we were invited to go on a boat ride in the Gulf. It was undoubtedly bikini weather—for Vikki, not for me! We stopped on a little island only accessible by boat. We did some swimming, I tried to swim out to a dolphin that kept its distance, and we looked for shells. We saw no bugs and made sure we applied an enormous amount of sunscreen. On the way back to land, Vikki's back started to itch.

When I checked Vikki's back, there were hundreds of little red bumps. It looked like she had the measles. The sandflies had attacked her. Yes, those nasty little no-see-ums. We now pack bug spray in our beach bag. We have been told they do not like lavender, and maybe we should invest in some. Bugs! Ugh! They are always around in paradise! People visiting paradise, similar to when we arrived, are not aware of these peculiarities. That's the price you pay! Welcome to Florida!

14

Health Care

One of the biggest problems when you move out of state is finding quality electricians, plumbers, a pool guy, an exterminator, and the list goes on. An even bigger issue is obtaining a physician. During our first three years, living in paradise, we found ourselves heading up north at least twice a year to continue with our regular doctor visits in our hometown. We made sure our physicals and dental checkups were done during our trips back up to Wisconsin. We finally decided it was time to accept the fact we needed to take care of these issues closer to our new home.

How do you find a good doctor or dentist? Part of that has to do with the type of insurance you have. I took basic dental insurance from my employer when I first got here, and it was an HMO. That was a mistake. We were given a good recommendation for a dentist, but we couldn't use them because their office did not take HMOs. So we found one that did. Well, that was not a very good experience. The dental office was a mess. The receptionist was friendly, but there were mounds of paper, reports, and confidential records all over her desk and countertops. It looked very disorganized and not very HIPPA. They wanted to put us on treatment plans and have us pay a significant amount of money up front. All we wanted was our biyearly cleaning. We left the office and waited until the next year, then I upgraded to the PPO, and we are able to go to a better dentist. Yay! Dentist! Check that off the list.

We researched many physicians for a regular doctor, and I was given a doctor that was about thirty minutes away and went for my annual physical. I was fifty-five at the time and by far the youngest person in the waiting room. When I had my appointment, the first thing my doctor asked me was what I was doing there. I'm in good health, and I said, "I just need to do my yearly physical." It was January.

It was a short visit. I was given a different clinic to have some blood work done, and I made an appointment for the next year. My blood work completed, and the results were sent to the physician's office shortly after that. I received a call from the doctor's office in July! They stated there was something in my blood work that they were concerned about, and they asked me to redo the test to confirm the results.

Well, WTF! That blood test was seven months ago. They were checking it now? I took the tests again. Everything was normal. I found a new doctor. Check off *doctor* from our to-do list.

Everything is trial and error down here; you receive recommendations where some are good and some are not. My wife found her doctor through a recommendation from the secretary at our school. So far, so good. I think we finally have our physician and dentist figured out. Yay! Now my wife needs to find a beautician!

So what do we do when we have an emergency, a medical emergency? We jump in the car and take our loved one to the local emergency room. Most of us who grew up in the communities we live in know exactly where that hospital is. We may have been there before as a patient or just a visitor. Regardless, we're familiar with it. We know what's positive, and we know their shortcomings. Whatever the case, we're comfortable going to that venue for help.

Moving to Florida has complicated that experience for Vikki and me. We're not medical test subjects. By that I mean we're in good health and are not on a long list of medications or any for that matter. We've heard horror stories about the health care options in Florida. There's a wide gap between excellence and mediocrity with health care here. There are far too many facilities falling below acceptable standards. A one out of five rating is not an acceptable facility to frequent.

When Vikki was stricken with a health concern, we experienced both spectrums in a relatively short period. She was suffering some stomach pains, urinary issues, lack of appetite, and a bloated abdomen. She went to her regular physician, who was not available, so she saw the nurse practitioner. Whatever Vikki told the nurse practitioner, they thought her problem might be an issue for a urologist, so they scheduled a CAT scan and set up an appointment with a specialist.

The Urologist diagnosed kidney stones, gave her a prescription for pain and two medications for a bacterial infection. She just got sicker, so another appointment with the Urologist and a second, more comprehensive CAT scan was scheduled. She was having severe pain in her lower right abdomen, but the apparent stones were on the left side. This abnormality completely baffled the urologist, and he hoped that the second CAT scan with contrast would help identify the issue. He advised that if the pain persisted or she got tired of it, she could go to the ER. The ER would get the tests done a lot quicker and could admit her and provide her with stronger pain meds. So we went home. She continued to suffer from severe abdominal pain, no appetite, and lack of any energy over the weekend.

The thought of trying to force down two quarts of chalky white, distasteful barium for a second CAT scan and continued discomfort finally convinced her to visit one of the local emergency rooms. It wasn't the extreme pain and discomfort she experienced for the past week that finally put her over the edge; it was the act of drinking the barium. We live in a small community. The hospital that is less than two miles from our house is one of the lowest rated in our area, recently earning a 1 out of 5. So our next option was a hospital ten miles away. We later learned this facility also earned a 1 out of 5 rating.

Emergency rooms are never fun, usually busy, have a mix of questionable characters in the lobby, but usually clean and somewhat organized. This was an older hospital. The lobby area seemed like disorganized chaos, but they got the job done. Once we checked in and they knew we had insurance, Vikki was whisked away for a variety of tests. Someone from billing found me and got my $200 copay right away. Because we were insured and could pay right away, we received a 10 percent discount! We arrived at 8:00 p.m., they did an excellent job of getting Vikki's test results, and by 10:30 p.m. we were meeting with the ER doctor.

In the meantime, I was by myself in the waiting room, I had no idea where Vikki was, and no one was communicating with me. I did have the pleasure of sitting next to a patient who had a Crohn's flare-up because he was out drinking with his mom earlier in the evening. They were both under the influence, and he was puking in a bedpan right next to me—thank you for that! What an experience!

When the ER doctor took us to another private little area, away from the craziness of the ER waiting room, she informed us that Vikki had a ruptured appendix with an abscess. The ER doctor advised us that the on-call surgeon would be with us shortly to prepare her for the surgery. Vikki was provided an IV for some nutrition. She had not eaten in a week and was given something for the pain. (The puking Crohn's guy was now right next to us separated by a curtain—with his mom. Oh my!)

Two hours later, after no contact with anyone, I found an orderly because Vikki needed to use the bathroom. That reminded everyone that the patient with the ruptured (life-threatening) appendix was still there. They put us in another curtained area, put some antibiotics in her now, and asked if we saw the surgeon yet. We hadn't; they said he would be here soon, so they checked us in and told us what would happen with the surgery.

Finally, she was being taken care of, or so we thought! We went up to a room to get her comfortable. The nurse asked us what we were doing there. Our response? "We have no idea, except that Vikki has a life-threatening situation!" Our nurse said, "Don't worry I'll call the doctor right now and find out what's going on."

She returned thirty minutes later with a look of discontent on her face. She was upset. The on-call surgeon did not want to come in; it was now 1:30 a.m. He said he would be there at 7:00 am, put her on antibiotics, and told the nurse he was NOT entirely sure the appendix had ruptured, and he would drain the fluid in the morning and decide what to do.

Our nurse started to make Vikki comfortable. Vikki had to use the bathroom, and the nurse opened the door to the bathroom in the room and almost barfed. The bathroom was a mess. The nurse then went and laid sheets and towels on the floor so Vikki could go in. Vikki was still in pain, so our nurse went to call the doctor one more time to beg him to come in. He was the doctor on call; it was kind of his job!

It was now 2:15 a.m. Vikki's appendix had burst some time ago. The doctor decided not to come in, so our nurse told us that we should leave. Yes, you heard that correctly. Our nurse had just told us to get out! She said that Vikki needed help. The physician and the hospital were not providing that help.

"Get out!" She told us to leave the hospital and this county; she suggested a hospital a mere fifty-three miles from our current location.

We took the nurse's advice, and I drove my wife, with a burst appendix, a life-threatening problem to a hospital at least an hour's drive away. Fortunately at two thirty in the morning, hwy 41 was not very busy. I'm not sure what the speed limit is on that road, but I know I wasn't following it. The hospital we traveled to had a rating of 5 out of 5. The ER doctor was not very happy to hear that we had left another hospital. We explained that we were not getting the treatment needed for Vikki's ruptured appendix. I think he was reluctant to believe us until Vikki went through her second contrast CT scan in six hours. Patients are not supposed to have more than one CT scan in a twenty-four hour period but we did not have the information needed when we bolted out of the first hospital. After our new ER doctor received the information confirming the ruptured appendix he apologetically told Vikki, "It is a very good thing you did not go home." Vikki was promptly scheduled for surgery and getting the help she needed. Our doctor there was terrific, and Vikki's life-threatening illness was over!

After the incident was over, I called the original hospital to find out who the physician on call was and attempted to make a complaint. I was told I should call the chief medical officer and have that discussion. I was transferred to the administration office; it was there I learned that they were currently without a chief medical officer. The current one retired, and there was a search for a new one. I was given the surgeon's name but also told it was not the surgeon at fault here. It was a problem within the hospital itself and the way they dealt with Vikki's issue. They will investigate and get back to me at a later date with their findings. That report has yet to be provided to me.

Now in my opinion it was the holiday season. I believe our surgeon may have had a few too many glasses of wine or eggnog and didn't feel he should come in. Our nurse may have suspected this, and that is why she was so adamant that we go somewhere else. Now I certainly could be wrong. Maybe he was just old and tired and thought this could wait. The ER doctor told us at 10:30 p.m. it was a ruptured appendix. We still never found out what time it burst. Dealing with this emergency was a stressful and confusing situation.

So the bottom line is, no matter if you need a doctor at the current time, research, research, research for the best place for you and your family. Hopefully, if we ever have a need for an emergency visit in the future, we can make it to that hospital outside of Charlotte County.

Vikki still needs to find a beautician!

15

Building on a Sandbar

The year 2008 was terrible financially in the United States. The housing crash at that time devastated Florida. The housing market came crashing down. Foreclosures skyrocketed, many developing neighborhoods stopped building, and people lost their homes and their dreams. Homes valued at $400,000 were being sold for a fraction of the cost, if they could sell them at all. Before the crash, the states of California and Florida saw home values climb 20 percent a year. When the market collapsed, so did a lot of dreams.

Fast-forward to 2015, Vikki and I had left Lakeland and were renting in Punta Gorda. This quiet little community was going to be our new home, so it was time to search for the house of our dreams. A realtor was recommended, we made contact, and we began our search. We were looking for a modest home, with our number one requirement, a pool. Another condition was to be relatively close to where we worked. A place close to the beach would've been ideal, but with our jobs in Punta Gorda, the nearest beach was Boca Grande or Englewood. We were not willing to drive an hour to get to work, so we kept our search close to our employment.

We went through a great number of properties and felt like we were on an episode of *House Hunters*. We tried to stay away from foreclosures and houses that had been on the market for a long period of time. One house we looked at appeared to be on a canal. It looked nice, relatively new build, and it had a unique pool. The canal was just a spillway with stagnant water, a mosquito sanctuary, and the price was a little higher than we expected, so we moved on. The next property we looked at was intriguing. It was in our price range, listed with a pool, and had a favorable location. Upon our arrival, the outside looked appealing, but then we went inside. The home had recently been bug bombed because it had been on the market for a while. There were dead critters of various shapes and sizes all over the place. When we went to look at the pool, the heating unit was missing many of its necessary parts. The water in the pool was dark green, with algae mounds floating across the top. Obviously this property was not our idea of a dream house!

We learned to be cognizant of the build date as we toured properties. "Chinese" drywall was prevalent during building from 2001–2009. The drywall was defective and would release a rotten egg smell that caused residents to encounter respiratory issues. We had never heard of Chinese drywall, so thankfully our realtor filled us in and helped us avoid that debacle. Some very questionable work took place, especially in Florida. During that time frame, the housing market was booming, and adherence to codes were often overlooked or disregarded.

We had built a home in Wisconsin, so after checking out so many questionable properties, we decided to pursue a new build. There were many developments and small gated communities popping up everywhere. Some were golf communities, with houses that had higher price tags. With the higher asking price were some great amenities, but also higher than what we were willing to pay. That's when we discovered Express Homes, a division of D. R. Horton. We set up an appointment to check out this new development less than a mile from the school where I would be working. We had been working with the Patterson Group, a highly regarded reality service, so we asked our realtor to attend the meeting with us. We had done our research on D. R. Horton, checked out the reviews, both positive and negative. Needless to say, we had a lot of questions, and our realtor was extremely helpful.

It was a new development, and the homes were going up pretty fast with a very positive price point. The primary concern became whether or not we could put in a pool. We had visited some of these developments and personal pools were not allowed. Many of them started at a base price, and you picked out everything from countertops to light fixtures. You could upgrade the type of appliances, flooring, cabinets, and hardware; everything could be upgraded, for a price. This process often puts the buyer way over budget, and you can end up with something you struggle to afford. Express Homes is a great concept, just a few choices, keep it simple, and keep the price point down. We were given four models to choose from depending on square footage. We were told that because of their no upgrade policy, they could build the houses quicker and generally within three to four months. Any changes, including adding the pool had to wait until after the house was yours. Our salesman, had a favorite quote: once you take ownership you can "make it your own!"

The intent is good, but a little understanding or willingness to communicate and work together could've kept our out-of-pocket expenses lower after we moved in. For example, we wanted to paint the walls before they put in the flooring. They used a builder's-grade paint that was precisely that, builder's grade, no gloss, all the same color. We knew we were going to repaint the entire interior. When we built our home in Wisconsin, our builder told us how much time we had before the flooring went in and we were allowed to paint. Express Homes? After you take ownership, "make it your own!"

The backyard had an in-ground sprinkler system. We had applied for permission from the association to put in a pool. We were going to have the hole dug immediately after we purchased the house—you know, "make it your own." It would've been very cost effective for us to change the layout of the irrigation lines in the backyard to accommodate where the pool would be placed. The builder said yes, of course, after ownership!

We were looking over the building schematic and saw that they were putting in an outside outlet in the lanai. They were putting it in the wrong place, and we asked—very nicely, I might add. They did *not* move it! Denied again. The unwillingness to work with the homebuyer, the reluctance to make something right, or correct a problem were unfamiliar to us. When we brought up an issue to the builder that would save both parties money, it seemed insane to us that the corrections would not be made.

We decided to build; we found a great lot with a pond in the backyard, our salesman took our picture with a new SOLD sign, it was July 12. We were given a closing date of October 13! Vikki and I were excited. We were building in Florida, our home on the sandbar!

Why am I calling it a sandbar? Why? Because we can get six inches of rain on one afternoon and the ground is dry by the next day. Call it a sandbar or a sponge, whatever you wish, it doesn't matter. This state will be the first to disappear when the polar ice caps melt.

Remember when I told you that the crash of 2008 destroyed Florida's economy? Well, they don't want that happening again! We soon learned the true cost of buying a home on this sponge. We purchased two homes in Wisconsin over the course of our lives, each time the closing costs were between five hundred and fifteen hundred dollars. When we sold our house to move to Florida, without a realtor, the closing costs were less than four hundred dollars. As we started working on the finance papers for our Express Home, the closing costs were twelve thousand dollars! We were in shock. WTF!

The state of Florida had put measures in place not to be devastated again by a housing crash. There were multiple fees and taxes built into the closing costs to protect the banks. Title fees for both the homeowner and seller that the homeowner pays. WTF! Flood insurance and homeowners insurance were built into the closing costs, our salesman's commission, and a variety of other taxes and fees. WTF! It's part of the deal; we want a home in paradise, so we have to do it! Besides we would be homeowners in paradise in October, right?

We also learned two new acronyms, HOA and CDD. We had a covenant in our prior community "up North," but HOA and CDD were foreign terms to us. Our new community had an HOA, which is a homeowners' association, and that required a monthly fee. The HOA fee includes care for the community pool and lawn service. I would never have to cut my grass again! Yippie! That's a good thing because I didn't own a lawnmower anymore, and there wasn't enough room in the garage to store one anyway. With the HOA comes a rulebook with pages and pages of clarifications detailing things we can or cannot do. We are not allowed to plant a bush, move a plant, or put in a tree unless we get approval from the homeowner's board. No basketball hoops attached to the garage, and they can tell me when I can put up and have to take down my Christmas lights. We cannot have a clothesline, and people are not allowed to leave their golf carts in their driveway. There's a rule telling when and at what hours of the day to place my garbage can outside and bring them in, and God forbid I leave my garage door open! I'm not complaining; however, when we were waiting for approval to put in the pool, the HOA advisor was *not* a very pleasant person to deal with.

The only thing that Vikki wanted was a clothesline. She loves the smell of windblown clothing, and it keeps me from shrinking clothes when I attempt to help with laundry. There are some portable clotheslines that can be moved in and out of the ground. That would be perfect for us, but if we ask permission, we will get denied. That was until we found out about the Solar Rights Act. That Right supersedes any law, and the HOA cannot deny it. We have yet to take this action, but when we do it will undoubtedly cause a stir in the community. We are such rebels!

If you were a Seinfeld fan, then you remember a few episodes where Jerry visited his parents who lived in Florida. Jerry's dad was the president of the HOA, and as he was attempting to get reelected, he found himself in the middle of some neighborhood disputes. Never in my wildest dreams did I see myself in a community like the one portrayed on that show. Fantasy becomes a reality; I attended my first association meeting, and I was not disappointed.

When I came home from the meeting, I told Vikki that if I ever get like some of the people at that meeting, put a chicken around my neck and throw me in the pond (we have a neighborhood gator and gators love chicken). It was comical listening to the things that the residents complained about. The roads in the development are private, so they wanted speed bumps and speed limit signs. They always complain about the cost of the association fees, and they want to put things in the community that would cost more money. A speed limit sign would be meaningless on a private road. There's a community pool with a long list of rules on it, including no diving. One gentleman was adamant that new signs should be put up that say "no jumping" as well. Kids come to enjoy the pool with their grandma or grandpa, and God forbid they jump in the water and have some fun. Do you really think a sign is going to stop that? Maybe communicate with them and ask them nicely to jump in at a different spot. There were more complaints, and each one was sillier than the last, needless to say, I may not be attending any more of those meetings. WTF!

As the community is filling up, more and more of the responsibility is falling on people in the neighborhood to monitor and police. We now have a team of five that will travel around and make sure we are all in compliance because now they want to fine people. Recently we've been advised we will have a neighborhood watch program. It is a gated community. Are people seriously worried, or is this just another way to keep tabs on what people are doing? Oh well, whatever keeps them busy and happy.

The complaints were starting to heat up because at the latest meeting (I did not attend), the community was told the fees would be going up. Many of our residents are on fixed incomes, and causes the grumbling to get amplified. To be fair, when we signed our contract, our salesman told us we would have one fee. Like a lot of things we were told, it is changing. We now have to pay additional HOA fees for maintenance on a recreation center that hasn't even been built yet? Something does not quite add up for me on that one. WTF!

CDD, Community Development District, is another term for more taxing because it's like an additional tax every year. The state has to approve all these new communities to make it more difficult or to protect themselves from what happened in 2008. The infrastructure—roads, sidewalks, and streetlights—are the responsibility of the developer, who in turn passes it on to the community. That means, at tax time, we're saddled with another one-thousand dollar expense. It will take us twenty years to pay off the CDD debt. WTF! Vikki didn't hear the explanation during the sales pitch; she thought it was a one-year charge. Her jaw dropped when I explained we had nineteen more years to go. No worries, we're in paradise, and we're moving into our new home in October, right?

Our new home was going to be built only three-quarters of a mile from my new school. I went by it every day. In August and September I kept waiting to see construction begin. We were moving in on October 13, remember? In mid-September, we stopped in to talk to our sales guy and asked again about our home. Something always came up—weather delay, worker shortage, or some other delay—yet he continued to say it'll be finished close to the initial date. Even I know you cannot build a house in one month.

The house not being completed when were initially told was a concern for us. We were renting the home of a snowbird who would be coming down to stay sometime in late December. Finally construction began in the middle of October, and a closing date for December 21 looked promising. The closing process with D. R. Horton? Well, that is another story. It was one of the worst closing experiences Vikki, and I ever went through. Let me share a brief recap.

We were all set to close on December 21. We drove to Fort Myers to their office, a forty-five-minute drive away. As we were pulling in the lot, we received a phone call explaining to us that they were delaying our closing until the following day. They had put the wrong picture of the house on the appraisal. I said I'm in the parking lot; I have a picture of the house on my phone, I can email it to you. Not good enough. We drove back to our rental with no keys in hand. As we pulled into the parking lot of D. R. Horton to close the next day, we received another call with another concern. This time I said, "Vikki, we're going in!"

We waited in the office for six hours as we forced them to process our paperwork. It was December 22. We were moving in *today*—or so we thought.

We had people waiting at the new place with our packed up Penske truck. (remember, no more U-Hauls for us!) After an exhausting day at D. R. Horton, we were still not allowed to move in until December 23. Our final paperwork wouldn't be done until then. However, we managed to get "permission" to unload our rental truck into the garage only. We were given "our" keys, so we had access to the entire property. The regular salesman was unavailable, so another person in the office felt sorry for us and slipped us the keys. We took advantage of this generosity and moved all our stuff into the house. As we were moving things in and placing it in the rooms where we wanted it, we felt like we were doing something wrong. This was our home. We hadn't officially closed, and we wanted to stay in the house overnight. We aren't that rebellious, and we were nervous that someone would call the police on us. That was even before our community started their neighborhood watch program. We stayed until early in the morning and then spent the night back in our rental. We had already done a final cleaning and exited from the rental. Now Vikki had to clean it all over again, rewash the bedding, sterilize the bathroom, every area we occupied. Just more delays before we could finally relax in our own home.

On December 23, we officially closed. We had scheduled and rescheduled a trip back home to Wisconsin for the holidays that year. We spent a glorious twelve hours in our new house and then not again until the New Year!

In hindsight, if we knew closing was going to be so close to Christmas, we would have canceled those plans and stayed in Florida to get our house in order.

Don't get me wrong, we love our new home, the community, and our neighbors, but the sales process, closing, and the misinformation along the way made our joyous process quite a nightmare.

16

Plumbers, Mechanics, Electricians—
Oh My!

Our house on the sandbar, or sponge, however you want to look at it was complete. We were homeowners in the Sunshine State. Living and owning a home in Florida means that at some point we will need a plumber, an electrician, a landscaper, or a mechanic. If you're like me, you rely on recommendations from your friends. When you're new to an area, you may not have those reliable and trustworthy contacts yet.

We thought our building experience was terrible. Our friends living in a popular beach community were building a sizeable property on the intercoastal. Their house is a beautiful home with many of those impressive upgrades that were not available to Vikki and me. Like most stories I have heard of people building or having some major remodeling done. They've had numerous delays and minimal explanations for them. After more than a year they are finally settled into their new home.

Contractors have so much work available they often don't care about their reputation. People in a hurry will employ them regardless of any negative reviews. Contractors hire available subcontractors; as much as they would like to find someone and continue hiring them, these subcontractors go where the money is. One of the reasons our house was not done by the original date was because the crews that were putting in the concrete and doing the masonry had left D. R. Horton to go work on a project paying more money.

When you have someone start your project, they often start more than one at the same time. They get to yours when it is convenient. When the weather is gorgeous and great for fishing, the crew may take a day off. There's no sense of urgency. They probably take a considerable down payment for your project, and they'll finish on their timeline.

Many times when you're attempting to do a project, and you're looking for quotes, you can call six different people to quote it, and no one shows up. Or maybe one person shows up, and you go with them because they answered your call. After a hurricane, problems finding contractors are amplified.

I attended a Chamber of Commerce luncheon when we first moved to Punta Gorda. I was sitting at a table with a gentleman that had started his own heating/cooling company. He did a lot of work on air conditioning units. He told us how he moved from Michigan and took a job working for a plumbing company. He would get a call to go to the residence of an elderly person who was experiencing a problem with a faucet. The project could be a quick fix, change out a washer, less than thirty minutes and out the door. The company often overcharged for the part and for their time.

After a few months, he started his own business. He told us that there is so much work to do and there are so many people that word of mouth and repeat business is not a concern for these companies or for many private contractors. This lack of follow-up can be very frustrating to homeowners who are looking to make improvements or repair damage. When you move from a community where you knew everyone, where the quality of the work was important, it is hard to get accustomed to the lack of follow through.

It is essential to find a network of people that help share information on quality contractors. There are a lot of good and conscientious people out there, and it is nice to reward them with referrals. Our gated community now has a Facebook page that provides recommendations for quality contractors. Thank goodness!

17

Honey, We Have Visitors

Florida is a destination and a vacation spot. The difficulty for most people when planning a vacation is, where will they stay? Most of the time they're visiting to get away from the terrible winter weather, which puts them right in *the* season. The cost of a hotel or a condo rental would cover one or two mortgage payments back home. The first thought is, "Who do we know that lives in Florida?"

We have stayed with many friends over the years, and it's certainly a great friend's benefit to have when traveling. It's especially great when there's a reciprocal arrangement. As soon as our friends and acquaintances realized that Vikki and I now live in Florida, the frequency of people requesting to visit skyrocketed! Even when we were renting a small apartment in Lakeland, the requests to come were continuous. Once we built our house, it became impossible to keep up with the many inquiries without a system in place.

Vikki has a planner that's just for visitors. When family or close friends are trying to schedule a visit, she has that planner close at hand to help keep things organized and to prevent us from becoming overwhelmed or overbooked (this has happened twice so far). One of our visitors altered their plans at the last moment, we had to push them out early because more guests were on the way. Vikki actually said to them "it's time to leave!" That was a bit of an anomaly. We look forward to having our family and friends come and enjoy all the amenities that paradise (Florida) provides.

Our family visiting is always the priority. We say come down, put your feet up, enjoy the pool, use the car, pretend you're at an all-inclusive resort. I'll grill and make you a wicked rum punch (the house specialty). With our out-of-state friends, it's a little different dynamic. They're coming for vacation. Vikki and I live here, and we're still working. Often our friends want to go out at night, visit attractions, or head to the beach. They want those plans to include us. However, we have to worry about our work schedules and certainly our own "vacation funds." We love to share in some of their vacation experiences; however, if we don't pace ourselves, we end up tired, run-down, and low on funds.

Friends that have been in your life for a long time are usually pretty aware of the responsibilities people have as residents of paradise. If they've had a grandparent or relative that lived in this state at one time or another, they have probably heard of the cost of living in Florida. Many of those visitors have us take them to the grocery store, and they load up on the food they want to have during the week at their expense.

It gets crazy when you start hearing from people you haven't spoken to in twenty years. Sure they may be a friend on some social media site, maybe a former classmate from forty years ago that hasn't communicated with you since graduation or who is an acquaintance at best. Hopefully, Vikki's planner is "full" for the week they're thinking about coming down, or we're out of town visiting our northern friends—is that bad?

A few tips to those that are lodging with "old friends" on vacation.

- Fly into the closest airport if you expect them to pick you up.
- Plan your excursions. Ask but don't expect the hosts to go with you all of the time.
- Head to the grocery store for things you enjoy.
- Buy them a drink or two!
- On your last day, take the sheets off the bed (much appreciated).
- Enjoy & Relax!

We have always had a great time with all our visitors, and we always look forward to showing off our town! We will certainly welcome you to Florida. Most importantly, relax, kick-back, and remember to have a great time!

18

Day Drinking

Hold onto your hats for this chapter, or your drinks, whichever you value more. Wisconsin is known for its drinking. There are breweries on every corner, triple and double bubble events during happy hour, and boozy woozy. You may not be familiar with those terms (check the glossary), but all you need to know is that Wisconsin knows how to drink!

There's no way Florida could be worse, or better, depending on your perspective regarding alcohol consumption. Our experience in Lakeland wasn't indicative of what takes place in Florida. We lived in an apartment, and we didn't know our neighbors. We weren't included in any after school activities with the staff at the school where we worked, and people didn't seem very friendly at the establishments we visited. As I think back on those experiences, maybe they thought we were snowbirds and saw us as invaders.

Then we moved to the coast, to Punta Gorda, the best-kept secret in Florida. It was the first day of my new job and it was getting close to the end of the day. The day ended at 2:45 pm. One of the staff invited Vikki and me to the Celtic Ray after work. What! Is this happening? We haven't even been here an entire day, and we were invited to a social activity? The Celtic Ray is an old Irish Pub located in downtown Punta Gorda. We arrived at 3:00 p.m., and it was packed! Again, I said it was 3:00 p.m.! Happy hour began at 2:00 p.m. Whaaat? In Wisconsin happy hour generally started at

4:00 p.m., and some establishments began at 5:00 p.m. That was the first sign things were a little different in paradise. Happy hour Friday, after the completion of the school day, became a weekly event.

When we moved into our new home, most of the neighbors were retired and primarily from the East Coast. We found out quickly that if you went to visit a neighbor at 11:00 a.m., you were getting offered a beer. If they came to visit you, there's an unwritten friendly expectation to reciprocate.

Day drinking can happen at any time. In a community full of retired people where every day is a weekend, unless you're working, there is always the possibility you could be drinking before noon. When the libation process begins before noon, you often find yourself asleep on your couch before dinnertime. The reality around town is that many of the bars and restaurants are empty and closed by 10:00 p.m. In Punta Gorda, a local joke is that midnight is considered 9:00 p.m. When you start drinking in the morning, 9:00 p.m. is pretty late. There are undoubtedly some establishments that provide live music and activity all throughout the evening. There is usually a good Irish band at the Celtic Ray, and Dean's South of the Border is always rocking until the wee hours of the morning. The clientele that is still out after 10:00 p.m. naturally didn't start at ten in the morning, and they are well under the age of retirement.

The liquor laws are crazy all over the state. Every county has different ordinances when it comes to alcohol sales and consumption. Desoto County, for example, is a dry county on Sundays. You cannot get a drink at a restaurant or the local pub on Sunday in that county. In contrast, the county just south of us just extended weekend bar closing time to 3:00 a.m.! In Polk County, the bars may close at 2:00 a.m., and if you can find them, there are drive-through liquor stores. After a night in the pub, the last call is given, the lights come on, and you drive home. If you are still thirsty, there it is, open all night—the drive-through liquor store. WTF!

In general, it's pretty expensive to drink in the beach communities. The establishments have fancy drinks and overprice them for the tourists, the deals in the off-season are much better. Factor in the drinking and driving laws, it's just easier to have a few in the neighborhood. Sometimes a few early drinks lead to more, and before you know it you're on that couch at 6:00 p.m. At least you're not on the road and a danger to anyone! In paradise, where it's always five o'clock somewhere, it doesn't even matter if it's five o'clock. Enjoy the libations any time of day, guilt-free. Be sure to have Uber on speed dial if necessary.

19

All Hail Publix

Publix is the largest and most famous grocery store chain in Florida. Everyone loves Publix! George Jenkins, from Lakeland, Florida (yes that is the name of the high school I worked at) started a small grocery store back in his youth that has expanded throughout the state of Florida. From the Panhandle to Key West, the most famous grocery store chain in Florida is Publix. There are two things you do not bad-mouth in Florida. You cannot say anything negative about Mickey Mouse or Disney, and you cannot talk negatively about Publix.

On the positive side, the Publix Corporation donates a size-able amount of money and resources to the communities where they're located. That means every town in Florida benefits from the presence of Publix because every city has at least one of these estab-lishments. Punta Gorda with seventeen thousand residents has two Publix stores, and they're always busy. The best time to go to Publix is Saturday night or late Sunday afternoon. If you try to go during the day, remember all those drivers that need booster seats are shop-ping at that time. Watch out for senior citizen days. Most are over fifty-five, so I guess we qualify—but stay clear!

The first time I heard the acronym BOGO, which means "buy one, get one," was at a Publix. Every week Publix has new BOGO items. If you shop at Publix and buy the BOGO items, you can do a pretty good job of saving money. Vikki and I like to buy our produce and meat at Publix. The quality of these products is much better than our other option for groceries. Even, for the name-brand items and paper products, we can usually do better when it's a BOGO item!

Publix is widely known for their deli and their Boar's Head meats. The deli and bakery at Publix are outstanding and known throughout Florida for their sub sandwiches. Delicious! Vikki and I often go to Publix for the rotisserie or fried chicken, and if you're are a seafood fan, their sushi is fresh and as tasty as any restaurant. For those that are big sushi fans, Publix has five-dollar sushi days on Wednesday—you will not be disappointed!

My dad was a grocery store manager, and I worked for him in my youth. My dad could've been George Jenkins. He was all about customer service, and he would do whatever he needed to do to keep a customer happy. I remember working for my dad, as a young man. One of my first jobs was bagging groceries and carrying the bags out for the customers. Publix is the only grocery store I have seen that still provides that service. I always take out my own groceries, but when the bagger at Publix asks me if they can take out my groceries, it's a nice gesture that has lasted over time. I think they want to get outside and enjoy paradise. They also are not allowed to take tips. Publix wants to provide the best customer service possible. That is exactly what they do!

Publix does offer a great grocery shopping experience. My dad, who passed away in 2016, would have loved Publix! When we shop there, I witness the awesome customer service and small-town feel, it's like I'm in my dad's store and he'll come and help pack up my groceries. Thank you, Publix!

20

Florida "Winter"

When you tell people that you're moving to Florida, one of the first questions they ask you is if you have spent a summer in the state? Not just a week or two when you were on vacation and enjoying the beach or the resort pool but an actual summer.

I'm not going to lie; it is *hot*! The humidity is brutal! The rain is daily during the summer season. Vikki and I said when we move to Florida we will have a pool! Nothing cools you off like a dip in the pool. When you're at the beach, or on the coast, there is often a gentle breeze off the water that allows you to catch that tan (or burn in my case) and not be subjected to the oppressive heat. Fair warning, though, when you leave the beach and head to your car in the parking lot, it will be a sweltering, dripping-sweat kind of *hot*! Your car will feel like an oven, and you'll need oven mitts to handle your steering wheel. That's the main reason why cars manufactured for Florida already have tinted windows. Locals keep windshield shades in their car to pop up on their dashboard when they park. Many have cloth steering wheel covers as well. The struggle is real!

When I take off on my twenty to thirty-mile bike rides in the summer, I pack an extra bottle of water, two on the frame and one in my jersey. The heat index is always upward of 105 degrees. My school year starts in August, and as I have stated before, I have no gymnasium! It can sometimes be unbearable. Can I hear a WTF!

That means all my classes are outside on a basketball court or an open field. That means *no shade*! During August and September, I have to change my T-shirt after every class period. Even if all I'm doing is standing and monitoring the class, my shirt is drenched by the time the class is over. I stop in the bathroom between classes and take what my Polish friend says is a "Polish shower." Wipe down with a towel, apply deodorant, put on a clean T-shirt, and spray with Axe. (I never really used Axe, that was his idea.) Even though he is Polish, I still want to try and stay politically correct. Can I call it a Polish shower?

The air-conditioning unit in our house is turned on in late May and runs pretty steady through October. We have a cage (screen) around our pool area that cuts out some of the UV rays and keeps the pool deck cooler than outside. We have a fan in the lanai that helps keep the air moving, and Vikki, and I spend most of our time by the pool during our Florida-winter, as we like to call it. Our doors and windows will be locked down tight to keep the precious AC in the house during the Florida-winter months. Once the dew point drops in late October, the doors and windows are open until the next June. Regardless of what month it is, I don't know why we even have a living room, we live on our lanai, something we certainly could not do in Wisconsin.

With the high humidity and dew point also comes the afternoon tropical rain shower. Checking the "feels like" temperature, which factors in the dew point or moisture, is now part of our daily routine. The rainy season moves in almost like clockwork the first week of June. During this week, it constantly rains with very little let-up. After that initial week of tropical rains, the days become sunny, with a spot shower or downpour every afternoon right around 3:00 p.m. When I say downpour, I mean a torrential rainfall that could dump one to three inches in less than an hour. These showers are often accompanied by hundreds of lightning strikes and booming thunder. Sometimes the thunder is so frightening we even jump out of our seats inside the house. Nature is always reminding us who is in charge. The sun comes back out, and in a few hours, the sponge that is the state of Florida soaks up the water and the lawn is dry once again. These rains usually come late in the afternoon and do not mess up your beach day plans.

21

Walter

Let me tell you a story about my grumpy neighbor. Let's just call him Russ. Russ moved into the development a few months before we did, a native of New York. His only real flaw is that he's a Buffalo Bills fan. To help you understand Russ, if you've ever seen a Jeff Dunham special (the ventriloquist comedian), Russ is Walter, or Walter is Russ; the two characters are interchangeable. Russ would be happy if he had a Genesee beer and a real New York cinnamon roll. He often complains that he can't find a good cinnamon roll in this state. He complains a lot about everything, but a real cinnamon roll would help. I feel his pain; we can't find fresh Johnsonville Summer Sausage, New Glarus Beer, or squeaky cheese curds here either.

Russ was the first person to introduce Vikki and me to day drinking. We were here one day when Russ walked over with three beers in his hand welcoming us to our new home. I have since put a refrigerator fully stocked with local beer in the lanai right next to the pool—Vikki and I are prepared. If we go to Russ's house, his specialty, along with handing me a beer, is making frozen margaritas. If the one beer turns into two or three, Russ's "Walter" comes out! That's when it gets fun. Russ will talk about his desire to go back to New York State, how he despises the weather, the traffic, and all the people. Russ has seen a few snakes, and his reaction to those nasty creatures is priceless. Then there was the time he had a fraaag in his toilet—that was quite the conversation!

Russ comes across like a grumpy old man, but like Walter, I think it's his schtick. He's a lovable guy and makes us all laugh. Russ talks of moving back to New York part-time during the summer months. That'd require leaving his wife to fend for herself so he can escape the heat. His wife, like us, has no desire to head back north. Russ is never going to move back. As much as he complains, there's no way he's paying property taxes in two states! All our visitors love Russ. It may be because Russ has a dog named "Boonie" who loves everyone. When we talk to friends and family about our neighbor, they always ask, "Is that the one that brings the margaritas over?"

Our grumpy neighbor just hasn't learned to embrace the drivers, the bugs, the heat, the fraaags, or the craziness that is the Sunshine State. WTF! No worries, I would venture to guess that regardless of the Florida community you would move into - you will find your own "Walter".

22

Irma, You B——

I previously mentioned some of the crazy weather we deal with in paradise. Nothing is more feared or taken for granted as a *hurricane*. Hurricanes are measured by category, depending on wind speeds. A category 1 is nothing more than a strong wind with some rain. Most Floridians will have hurricane parties for anything under a category 4. A category 3 is still pretty wicked, 110–130 mph winds with the potential for quite a bit of flooding. Most of the roofs are "rated" for just under 200 mph winds, and pool cages are generally suitable for 150 mph, so why not throw a party, right? WTF!

That doesn't mean there won't be damage; it just makes people a little more comfortable than they should be.

Punta Gorda was devastated in 2004 when Hurricane Charley took a sharp turn off the Gulf and surprised the community. Residents were throwing hurricane parties because even though they were under a warning, Punta Gorda was not in the projected path. Vikki remembers watching that news coverage for hours. Little did we know it would be our future home! Through our travels around the town of Punta Gorda, we have heard the stories and have seen numerous pictures of the devastation. Despite the damage, Punta Gorda was like the Phoenix rising from the ashes to become something much better.

Hurricane Charley's is a favorite Raw Bar and Grill that is an example of rising from the ashes. It is located on the harbor and displays many pictures of the devastation, including a piece of plywood recovered from the hurricane that reads, "No Insurance, NEED FEMA, Send Help! You Loot, We Shoot." They serve a great rum punch as well.

During our first two years in Florida, the first in Lakeland and then the next in Punta Gorda, we experienced a few hurricane warnings that fizzled out or never materialized. Our first actual, wind blowing, rain-producing, damage-creating hurricane was Irma! Irma was massive. She covered the entire state and projections for points of impact changed hourly. At first, we were safe—well, relatively. We expected some wind and rain with a possible category 2 or 3 weather event—you know, party classification. As Irma traveled closer to the state, the outlook was looking a little bleaker. The strength started fluctuating between a category 4 or 5. Landfall was projected for a Saturday, and school was called off on the Thursday and Friday prior. When the severe weather looks imminent, they try to let you prepare as much as possible. Vikki and I watched the news for any sign that we should hunker down in our house or hit the road.

The first day off of school, Thursday, I put up our hurricane shutters. These shutters are long lengths of metal that screwed into the house to protect the windows. The house gets dark extremely fast when those panels go up, and they shut out all the light. The Thursday evening weather forecast was bleak. Our boys were watching the news from California, Las Vegas, and Milwaukee, and they started calling and begging us to flee! That evening, at 11:00 p.m., we decided we'd leave the next day at 5:00 a.m. We packed up our car with our important papers, extra gas, some food, and extra clothing. We have two bins filled with hurricane emergency supplies. One supply container held food, water, flashlights, batteries, a radio, candles, etc. The other container had room for our important papers and was stocked with extra clothing. We had a little Hyundai Elantra at the time, and every available space in the car was packed. At 5:00 a.m. on Friday we locked up the house, put up the final shutter, and hit the road.

We had prepared well for an eventual emergency. However, as we packed the car, we made one more trip to the local Walmart to pick up a few extra items. I grabbed the last pair of rubber boots in case of flooding; my flip-flops and sneakers would not be much help in a flood. We walked by the grocery department, and people were fighting over cases of water. The Walmart employee would bring out cases of water on a pallet, twenty-four bottles in a case. We witnessed people grabbing the cases off the pallet as it was pulled down the aisle. As one woman grabbed a case and put it in her cart, she turned to get another case, and the guy behind her grabbed the case out of her cart. There was a lot of yelling, pushing, and shoving for a few days. WTF! A scene right from the apocalyptic movies we enjoy.

Our first decision was to go to Tallahassee. Our oldest son had a friend who offered us some space in his apartment. Shortly after accepting that rescue offer, a cousin who lived there, in the same city, offered us a room. We decided to take the offer from family and hopefully be safe from the storm. We mapped out our route, hoping to stay off interstate 75 because reports were coming in that the gas stations were out of fuel and the traffic was moving very slowly. We took Hwy 19, through the beach communities of St. Petersburg, Clearwater, and Redington Beach. After the beach communities, it was two lanes and mostly rural. I'm not so sure this route was much better. We had good driving stretches at the speed limit and stretches where we crawled at a snail's pace. At one point we needed to gas up the car, and we chose to save our extra five gallons in our container for an emergency. That decision took us an hour out of our way to find the only station that still had gas. We waited in line for an hour, and as I was paying, the low tank warning lights were blinking on and off inside the station. There were soon to be a lot of very unhappy people. These lines were very reminiscent of the gas lines in the 1970s.

There were very few gas stations, and with the help of the Gas Buddy app, we knew who was out of gas and who still had some petrol. We love to watch apocalyptic movies, but again this trip made those movies seem closer to reality than we would have cared to think. Cars were pulled over at the side of the road with empty gas tanks, and people were hanging out on the side of the road waiting for any assistance. I feared that we'd end up stranded on a highway, in the boonies, in what would be one big parking lot. Our five-hour trip to Tallahassee took us eleven hours that day. We were exhausted yet ecstatic to get there!

In the meantime, our community was located in a red zone. That means we're in a flood zone and the first to be evacuated. It wasn't long after we left that Friday that our zone was required to vacate. When they tell you to evacuate, you are supposed to go. *No one* is coming to check to see if you left; many of our neighbors decided to stay. The problem with remaining is that if you did get flooded or you find yourself in a life-or-death situation, *nobody* was coming to help! That would've been enough for me to leave. We still had a few die-hard neighbors that hunkered in, but most of them were smart and evacuated at the very last minute. Irma was a crazy b—— and decided to follow us to Tallahassee. We had a beautiful day in Tallahassee on Saturday with our relatives. That evening the reports were looking bleak for the people in Tallahassee as well. The hurricane category was raised, and we made a decision late Saturday evening to leave Tallahassee on Sunday. We had to head further north as Irma was covering the entire state of Florida! WTF! We found and booked a hotel in Birmingham, Alabama. We jumped in the car for a five-hour trip to Birmingham that turned into nine. We weren't the only ones who decided to get out! To top it off, Vikki was having some intestinal problems, which meant frequent bathroom breaks! Those intestinal issues turned into that burst appendix you read about earlier.

Irma (that b——) hit that Sunday in Punta Gorda, drifted a little inland, and moved right up the center of the state. The downtown area of Punta Gorda had some flooding, but for the most part, Charlotte County fared better than anticipated. The school was out for that entire next week while efforts were made to restore power and clean up. Vikki and I left Birmingham and drove straight home that Tuesday after impact. The drive back was slightly better than the escape out. We did it in one day, and we were pleased when we returned to our home completely intact. A few bushes were bent over due to the wind damage, but that was the extent of our first real hurricane. We had minor flooding in our street and halfway up our driveway but nothing close to the house. We were very fortunate!

We have friends that live in Key West who waited almost two weeks to return home. We had just visited them the week prior, and many of the places we enjoyed during our stay there received significant damage. Our Key West friends had minor landscape damage, but all else was good. Many people experienced loss, but the response from those not affected was tremendous. People were gathering extra food and water and taking it to drop-off points. Those people that fought for cases of water right before the storm were giving it away afterward. We live in a crazy world!

So what did we learn from our first real hurricane threat? Our Express home was built to code and is pretty sturdy and able to withstand a category 4 hurricane. A 5? Not so sure. We did a pretty good job of preparing our hurricane tubs, but we probably need a little more water and food that's not perishable for the next hurricane season kit. We also need to add some warmer clothes in the kit as well. Flip-flops and tank tops don't always cut it. Finally, we are not going to do that drive ever again. There are just too many things that can go wrong, and our escape was stressful and nerve-racking. Our plan for the next major hurricane is to head to the Punta Gorda airport (less than two mile from our home). We will take a travel bag and get on the first flight to Anywhere, USA, preferably out of any storm path. If something happens and our home is lost, there's not much we would be able to do about it anyway. We might as well get out, enjoy ourselves and clean up when it's all over.

We're not big fans of hurricanes, but the alternative is subzero weather in Wisconsin, where it is possible to have snow from October to late April and a lack of sunshine throughout the winter months. So we'll take our chances and be prepared to throw a party for anything under a category 4 and get the hell out if it is higher than that!

Welcome to Florida!

23

The Water

There are many locations to choose from when you wish to relocate from a state with terrible winters. So why, other than our experiences from our youth, did we pick Florida? We had a list of criteria: Palm trees were a must—Florida had them. The fact that there is no state tax was a contributing factor but not a deal breaker—Florida, check! Sunshine and warmth for the majority of the year, again Florida hit the mark. There were a few other states in consideration for us, Texas, Nevada, So Carolina, and Arizona. However, Florida had an abundance of one thing these states did not have. Water!

Water, water, and more water! More specifically, the ocean, the Gulf, beaches, the water. And the most significant thing about all this water? It never freezes! The first year we lived in the state, we kept driving over bridges and marveling at the large bodies of water, and even better, the water never froze! Vikki and I visited the beach at least two times a month during our first year living in Florida and every time I jumped into the Gulf of Mexico. Yes, the water was a little cold in January, but if I tried that in Wisconsin, I would've been a popsicle!

We have friends that have boats, and we have been fortunate to take some trips with them and explore some islands only accessible by boat. We have seen sea life: dolphins, manatees, large sea turtles, and even sharks on these adventures. I enjoy and am grateful for those boat trips, but a boat is an item I will not ever purchase. They are a huge pain in the arse and quite expensive to maintain. One of our friends spends close to an hour cleaning up the boat, rinsing the salt water out of the motor, every time we come in from an excursion. There is a party going on in his house, and he is out there cleaning up, a necessity if he wants it to keep running.

Vikki and I will eventually get a water device, but ours will be a two-person kayak. Kayaking in Florida is awesome! We have kayaked on the intercoastal waters, which are usually calm, and the water is often clear enough to see creatures below the surface. We spent some time in Key West with friends, and they took us kayaking in an area filled with mangroves and shallow clear water. Doing anything on the water is very relaxing, and we can get a little exercise in a kayak.

SUP, dog? SUP stands for "stand-up paddleboard."

SUP is a crazy new activity taking place all over the country. This paddleboard is similar to a surfboard. You take it out into the water, and then you attempt to stand up on it. You can sit or kneel, but the actual experience is to stand. The only other tool you have is a paddle, so you stand up and paddle! The first time I tried this I was at a resort on Sanibel Island visiting friends who were enjoying the island. The resort had SUPs you could try out, and try them out we did!

It took about five or six wipeouts into the water before I got the hang of it. I believe by my third spill, the tide had gone out, the water was shallow and I landed directly on my tailbone! The drive home that day was not very pleasant. I had trouble sitting for a week. Once I got the hang of it, though, it was a pretty cool experience, just paddling along and looking at the water and what was below. The only tricky times were when a boat or Jet Ski would whiz by and create a wake. Learning to navigate the waves was another new trick. I think I could get into SUPing!

I have no qualms about kayaking or SUPing in the intercoastal waters or near the beach in the ocean or gulf. I have huge reservations about trying either one of these activities in a Florida river. Many people participate in these activities up and down the river, but I haven't lived here long enough to get comfortable with the gators! We may just reserve that venture for a time when we can use a glass-bottom see-through kayak. Except for eating gator bites at a local bar and grill, I don't need to be near those creatures.

Another awesome experience is saltwater fishing. I was fortunate to be a guest on a three-person saltwater fishing trip. I had fished very infrequently as a young lad, because my youth was filled with sports, so there was not an opportunity for me to hunt and fish. My dad enjoyed those activities, but they were always a bit too slow for me. I wanted to be active and moving; sitting on a dock or in a tree stand did not thrill me.

Fast-forward four or five decades and fishing seems a little more enjoyable, especially on someone else's boat and using someone else's equipment.

Our three-man fishing trip took us about six miles offshore, out in the Gulf of Mexico, and we were looking for grouper and snapper. These are two very delicious fish should we happen to catch any. Our guide was a seasoned veteran and had some key spots marked. It took us a little while to get our first nibble, but then the grouper started biting. We caught quite a few red grouper, but they were just under the size requirement, so back to the Gulf they went. It was still a blast to battle them and reel them in.

We wanted to bring something back with us, so we ventured a little further out and hit the spot where some snapper were biting. The snapper is a pretty fish and another good fighter. We ended up catching six of them. All of them were good sized, and we brought them home with us. I reeled in one fish that was putting up a good fight, and I thought I had a big grouper. I love grouper fillets and I was excited I could be grilling one of those bad boys for dinner. After a tenacious battle, I brought up a small ugly fish. Our guide said it was a mother-in-law fish. That wasn't the real name, but they nicknamed it that because it was so ugly. Good thing my mother-in-law isn't around to hear that! We threw that one back! Who wants another mother-in-law?

Our fishing party got together a few nights later with our spouses and enjoyed our saltwater dinner. The fillets were awesome, and the camaraderie was great. It just would've been nice to catch a few more.

If you live in Florida or just come for a visit, make sure you take time to enjoy the water. It is available 365 days a year, something not available the farther north you travel.

24

WTF! It Is Crazy Here

The only thing I can say is, it's Florida. Regardless of what part of the country you live in, you will often turn on your local news and hear some strange and bizarre news report from somewhere else in the United States. The stranger the story, the better the chance it has originated from the Sunshine State. Maybe it is because we're closer to the equator or because the bad stuff never freezes and goes away. Regardless, we're here to entertain and amaze. The following are a few stories, taken from the headlines, that caught our attention in Florida.

Most people have heard of The Villages, a fifty-five-and-older community in Sumter County a few miles east of Hwy 75 and north of Tampa. The Villages offer four unique communities, each with their little own little town square. It's a golf cart community, and you can find custom-made golf carts that look like '57 Chevys, Corvettes, fire trucks, or decked out promoting your favorite sports team—we saw a pretty cool Green Bay Packers cart—Go Packers! Some of these carts are even air-conditioned and have some quite elaborate coverings to protect the occupants from the rain. The price tags can be more than thirty thousand dollars.

In 2014, The Villages had a ratio of ten women for every man in the community. They made national news because a forty-nine-year-old man was arrested for having sex in the town square with his sixty-eight-year-old girlfriend. Immediately following that report, it was learned there was a huge black market in the community for Viagra.

The following stories all took place in 2017 in the state of Florida:

A Florida man, after visiting the Oyster Bar in Siesta Key, observed they had dollar bills stapled all over their walls. The bills were from patrons who wrote a note or their name on them to commemorate their visit. This man broke in after closing and took $150 worth of singles off the walls. He was arrested after visiting the local Publix for one of their famous Pub Subs. The employees were suspicious when they collected his payment in marked-up singles.

In June of 2017, a Piper PA 31 was attempting a night landing at a smaller airport. An eleven-foot, five-hundred-pound alligator jumped up and attacked the wing of the aircraft. The gator died immediately, and no injuries were reported from the pilot or passengers.

On texting and driving, currently, forty-three states in the Union have laws against texting and driving. Florida was about to become the forty-fourth state and help put an end to this dangerous and deadly practice. That is until Senator Rob Bradley cited worries about police invading driver's privacy and his fear that minorities could be treated unfairly. The bill has been pushed aside.

A Florida man spies a vehicle stranded on the side of the road and attempts to break in and steal the car. It was an unmarked county squad car with two officers inside. Can we say *unsuccessful?*

In Marion County, a man after being arrested stuffs $1,000 into his anus to hide it from the arresting deputies. Can we say *hemorrhoids?*

A fifty-three-year-old woman from Polk City was arrested for DUI while riding her horse down the road. She was also arrested for animal cruelty as she was putting the horse at risk. Her blood alcohol level was .161; the legal limit is .08.

Russian leader Vladimir Putin, in his most recent state of Russia address, uses a first strike nuclear simulation with Florida as the target WTF.

After Hurricane Irma, two men steal a metal power pole. They're caught driving down the road with the thirty-foot pole strapped to the top of their vehicle.

A Florida man calls 911 for a ride to Hooters. He got a ride all right, but his destination did not serve wings.

A Florida man in North Naples was dog sitting for a friend. While he was on the golf course, the dog was collecting golf balls. When the dog jumped in the water to cool down, a gator attacked him. The dog sitter jumped in the water to distract the gator. The dog got away with a bite to the leg and left the man in the water with the gator. The Naples man was able to back out of the water and get to safety.

During Easter dinner (2018), a woman in Altamonte Springs sprayed gasoline on her ex-boyfriend and set him on fire during dinner. October 2018 - Two middle school girls in Bartow, Florida (a small community just south of Lakeland) threatened to violently kill classmates and drink their blood. They had also planned to leave body parts at the school entrance.

And finally, in light of a recent school shooting in Florida, the legislature's answer is to arm teachers. The governor took five hundred million dollars out of the state's reserves to improve school safety. The biggest part of that bill is to train teachers to carry. The schools are poorly funded, teacher pay is in the bottom third of the country, and teachers cannot afford materials for their classrooms. However, we can find the time (143 hours of training) and money to have teachers carry a weapon. They're offering a bonus—maybe I can bump up my pay! WTF!

25

The Beach, Our Why

You've probably seen the Corona beer commercial with the slogan "Find Your Beach." That's what Vikki and I did. Before our final decision to move, we were visiting our son in California. I stopped in a bike shop and purchased a new jersey. The shop owner had an accent, and I asked where he moved from. He told us he had moved from Minnesota. Curious, I asked him why he relocated. He explained to us that he was only really living three months out of the year in Minnesota. The activities he loved were outside, and Minnesota weather, like Wisconsin kept him indoors for nine of those months. Vikki and I thought about his statement and realized it was true for us as well. We love the beach, and there certainly are not very many of them in Wisconsin.

Whatever your beach could be, define it and make your plan to live it! In our case, it was the actual beach. It wasn't just the warm weather, the endless summer, or the fact we would never have to shovel snow again that drew us to the Gulf Coast of Florida. It was always *the beach*!

When our sons, and their significant others, come down to visit (we have four of them), we try to plan one day for them to visit a beach. If they want shells, we head to Sanibel Island or Boca Grande. Boca Grande is better for shelling, but the restaurants on Sanibel and Captiva are unique and interesting to visit. If our boys want to hunt for shark teeth, there's no better place than Manasota Key Beach in

Venice. Most of the time, they want a more touristy beach, so we head to Fort Myers Beach or Siesta Key. Gilligan's, in Siesta Key, is an excellent place for a rum drink and a grouper sandwich if you head that way.

If you want a magnificent sunset, any of those beaches will do, but we enjoy Englewood Beach. It's the closest beach to our house, and the SandBar Tiki & Grill provides a great outdoor coastal atmosphere right across the street from our sunset viewing. If we're in the mood to drive, just north on Hwy 41 is Bradenton and Anna Maria Island. If we head to Ana Maria, we park by the Kokonut Hut. This establishment is right on the beach and has great cocktails and excellent food. If you are up to a little drive, Key West is truly a unique destination and has much to offer. While none of our children inherited the beach bug like their parents, they don't mind heading there for a few hours, especially if we're buying dinner later. They always ask us, "Why do you take the trouble to go to the beach when you have a nice pool?" Why? Because we can! The beach is always calling us!

Remember, I told you earlier that when our boys were young, we would save money for four years to go on a vacation that usually included a beach. Now we can be to the beach in under an hour and on less than a tank of gas. It is relaxing, plopping a chair in the sand, reading a book, looking for shells, or playing in the waves. Research shows that listening to the waves crashing onto the shore produces a calming effect in the brain. I have to admit; sunsets never cease to amaze Vikki and me. The two of us also collect refrigerator magnets when we travel. We look very hard for a magnet for each of the beach communities we visit. We have a refrigerator on our lanai, and our goal is to cover it with our travel destinations. We also have a sign in our house that reads, "The Beach—where doing absolutely nothing is doing something!"

Once we made up our minds to take the plunge and move to Florida, our life has been off the rails. The move, the new job, buying a house was a fast and furious endeavor. We certainly had some obstacles along the way, and we learned to navigate the intricacies of living in a new state. We gave up great jobs and a level of comfort in Wisconsin to take on our new challenges in Florida. We miss our close friends but they always have a place to visit. The path wasn't always smooth and at times we felt isolated like we were in the witness protection program, but it has been an adventure and continues to be so. We recently celebrated thirty-six years of marriage. When young couples ask us how we stayed together so long in this age of rinse-and-repeat marriages, Vikki always tells them that we decided long ago that life was an adventure and to have fun along the way. The key is to look at each moment, be it good, bad, or indifferent, that presents itself as an adventure. This change of lifestyle, this change of latitude has truly been an adventure, and we're better because of it.

The message here, if you're looking for one, is to follow your dream. If you talk about changing your current position in life, if you dream of packing up your life and changing your situation, do it! A little research may make the transition smoother. Maybe a little bit more time than we took (selling the house, accepting the job, and moving in a month) will make it easier. What you don't want is to look over at your seventy-year-old partner and wonder what could've been.

Despite the gators, the bugs, the Rebel flags, the tax collector, hurricanes, or the drivers that cannot see over the steering wheel, we love our new destination, new friends, and the adventures that we experience along the way.

"What's that, honey? Yeah, yeah, I'm coming."

The beach is calling!

ACKNOWLEDGMENTS

The process of bringing this project to completion could not have been done without the help of the one that went through it with me, my wife, Vikki Winkler. Thank you, sweetheart, for the good times, the journey itself, and the journey that still lies before us.

Vikki and I would like to say a special thanks to our children whose support of our journey to paradise helped to ease any apprehensions we may have had along the way. Bart and his wife Nikol; Brett, the man who reads over most of our work before submission, Brock and his wife Angie, along with our beautiful granddaughter, Sophia Ann Marie; and our youngest Brent.

The support, love, and encouragement shown by our parents as we looked for the best spot to settle in the Sunshine State. Jean Winkler, my mother, who is quite the traveler herself, and both of our fathers, Richard Winkler and Gerald "Bruno" Brunelli, who have both passed since the move. And we cannot forget Jackie Brunelli, my mother-in-law long since passed, who would have certainly enjoyed the destination we settled on.

Janice Church and Barb Mueller, both who made recommendations before we sent the manuscript to the printers.

Janie Clark, English teacher extraordinaire at FSWC, who provided some great advice that hopefully transferred into a more enjoyable read for everyone.

Lisa Provino and Jody Heady, two outstanding reading teachers in Lakeland that helped me survive my year teaching a subject that was foreign to me—intensive reading!

Roy Ramirez, a not-so starving artist, for designing an original cover that brings the book to life.

And for all of those individuals I did not name that have added to our adventures and Florida experiences. We will have many more WTF moments as our journey continues and we explore the state that has been built on a sandbar.

FLORIDA TERMINOLOGY

barnacles – This is a sea crustacean that attaches to everything that goes in the water: boats, rocks, boards, shells, etc. They are hard and pointy and will cause damage to the bottom of your feet should you step on them. (Right Brent!)

best friend - Anyone from your past who knows of your new Florida existence. They will search you out for a possible cheap vacation stay.

blue poles - It is colder in Wisconsin, so airport wheelchairs have blue poles, same color hair will occupy the chair.

boogie board - It's what the young kids at the beach throw down and jump on, skirting across the beach (not to be confused with a stand-up paddleboard).

boozy woozy - A raffle that usually takes place around the holidays in Wisconsin. A limited number of raffle tickets are sold, and winning tickets receive bottles of booze.

brackish water - Ugly brownish-looking water, a mixture of fresh-water rivers joining with the beautiful bluish-green saltwater of the Gulf.

canal - A waterway next to your property. If you have a boat, it allows access to a harbor, the Gulf, the Atlantic, or a causeway. It raises your property value and, of course, your homeowner's tax.

cracker - This is not a racist term, as it could be perceived that way in different parts of the country. It applies to anyone born and raised in Florida. *Cracker* comes from the early ranchers that would crack their whips to drive their cattle.

double bubble- During happy hour in Wisconsin, you buy one drink and get one free. Not prevalent in Florida.

flip-flops - Standard footwear, whether a tourist or a local. Socks are not required; open-toed and open-heeled is the only way to go.

FloGrown - Someone who was born and raised in Florida. Tolerant of snowbirds and transplants because of the cash they bring to the state. Always aware and often will remind you that you are not a native. Will probably have a FloGrown sticker on their pickup or tattooed somewhere on their body.

gawker - The driver that slows down to look at something located off the freeway, causing the fast-moving interstate to come to a complete standstill.

halfback - People that migrate from the North or East Coast, live in Florida, get tired of the humidity in the summer, and move to Tennessee, the Carolinas, or Kentucky, halfway back to their point of origin.

happy hour - A time to visit local pubs and get discounted drinks, approximately beginning at 4:00 p.m. up north, 2:00 p.m. in Florida, or noon, or 11:00 a.m., or 10:00 a.m. It's always five o'clock somewhere.

hopscotching - When a hurricane is forecasted and a Floridian hops from one part of the state to the other or to a bordering state to avoid the impending storm.

jetties - A breakwater constructed to protect the coast or inlets.

lanai - The area in the back of a house. Up north they would call it a patio or a deck. Lanais are often screened in (due to no-see-ums) and can include a pool.

mangroves - Trees native to Florida that help keep the coastline from slipping away. The gnarly root system that makes it extremely difficult to walk through. Protected—do not disturb or go to jail!

no-see-ums – More commonly known as sand flies. These are invisible teeny, tiny little insects that sting and cause itching. Very annoying and always around no matter the season.

Q-tips – A white-haired man wearing white shoes.

rednecks – Rural Floridians, usually drive a pickup, hate cyclists, and have gators and snakes as pets. Also good with any firearm.

red tide – Natural forming algae bloom that in high concentrations cause breathing problems for beachgoers. You can't see it, and it is not red. Also causes death to fish, which then accumulate on the beaches, making it unpleasant for sunbathers as well as sea-life.

red poles – Wheelchairs in Florida have red poles on them. You will see many of them should you prepare to board a flight out of Florida. The occupant usually has silver hair.

riptide – This is a current that flows in many different directions, causing significant problems on the beach for those swimming in the water. There are usually warnings when it is a problem for you as a beachgoer. Best advice? Do not jump in during this event.

seagrass – Seagrass is precisely what it sounds like—grass that grows in the sea, usually in shallow areas. Do not use your lawnmower.

seawall – The material that separates your property from the Gulf or the canal where you live. It prevents erosion of your backyard into the waterway.

sea spider – A nine-legged starfish, harmless to pick up, very cool to put on your head and let their legs snug your scalp. Please return to their natural habitat when you are finished playing with them, or you will receive a steep fine for removing them.

snowbirds – Usually over age 55 and a resident of a northern, eastern, or midwestern states, also includes Canadians. Temporary visitors that like to golf and help stimulate the state's economy. All members of the "I Hate Snow" club. A common cause of all traffic problems.

socks – These go on your feet when the temperature dips below sixty-five degrees. Should not be worn with sandals or flip-flops. (That doesn't mean you won't see it, though.)

squeaky cheese - Found fresh in Wisconsin. Cheese curds right from the factory—warm, squeaky, yellow, and delicious. Do not be fooled by advertising in Florida for Wisconsin cheese curds. They are often just fried mozzarella sticks (white cheese).

stand-up paddleboard - Often referred to as SUP. SUP is an impressive activity if you can get up on the board. If you are less than athletic, heading past middle age, or just clumsy, you may have trouble on this. An excellent way to traverse the waters in the many causeways of Florida. Especially fun to do where the water is clear; your vertical positioning allows you to see much of the unique sea life.

stingray shuffle - The process of sliding your feet when you enter the water on the Florida beaches. Shuffling helps kick up any sea creatures to prevent you from getting stung or bit.

tide pool - Can usually be found at low tide on rocky beaches. Water collects in small pools separate from the ocean or gulf when the flow goes out.

tiki bar - An outdoor bar with a thatched roof usually found next to the water, open-air places to relax and have a cocktail or a local craft brew. You can generally find an excellent grouper sandwich or gator bites as well. TT's Tiki is our favorite in Punta Gorda.

triple bubble - Aggressive bars in Wisconsin during happy hour, buy one, get two drinks free.

Winkler's Paradise Cove - The name we gave our house when visitors come for a retreat. Make sure you double check your reservation to avoid overbooking!